THE 12 MONTH WRITING CHALLENGE

Write and Publish 12 Books a Year

Copyright © 2022 by Ruth Barringham

Published in Australia

The author is the copyright owner of this work and no part may be reproduced by any process, nor may any other exclusive right be exercised without the permission of the Author.

This book is sold subject to the condition that it shall not, by way of trade or otherwise, be lent, re-sold, hired out, published electronically online or otherwise circulated without the Author's prior consent. All instances of copyright infringement will be dealt with to the full extent of the law.

The Author is not a lawyer or an accountant and does not intend to render legal, accounting or other professional advice within this book. No guarantees of income, sales or results are promised. It is recommended that users of this book seek legal, accounting and other independent professional business advice before starting any business or acting upon any advice given herein.

ISBN:	Paperback:	978-0-6454502-0-0
	Ebook	978-0-6454502-1-7

Book cover image courtesy of Mikołaj, Unsplash.com

Also by Ruth Barringham

How to Quit Smoking

How To Write An Article In 15 Minutes Or Less

Goodbye Writer's Block

7 Day Ebook Writing and Publishing System

Living The Laptop Lifestyle

Mission Critical for Life

Self Publish Worldwide

The Monthly Challenge Writing Series

Book 1 - Quick Cash Freelance Writing

Book 2 - Build A Lucrative Niche Website

Book 3 - Fast & Profitable Article Writing

Book 4 - The One Month Author

See more of my books on my website

https://ruthiswriting.com

Disclaimer:

The Author and Publisher have used their best efforts in preparing this book. The Author and Publisher make no representation or warranties with respect to the accuracy, applicability, fitness, or completeness of the contents of this book.

The Author is not a lawyer or an accountant and does not intend to render legal, accounting or other professional advice within this book. No guarantees of income, sales or results are promised. It is recommended that users of this book seek legal, accounting and other independent professional business advice before starting any business or acting upon any advice given herein.

The information contained in this book is strictly for information purposes. Therefore, if you wish to apply ideas contained in this book, you are taking full responsibility for your actions. Whilst we hope you find the contents of this book interesting and informative, the contents are for general information purposes only and do not constitute advice. We believe the contents to be true and accurate as at the date of writing but can give no assurances or warranty regarding the accuracy, currency or applicability of any of the contents in relation to specific situations and particular circumstances.

This book is not intended to be a source for advice, and thus the reader should not rely on any information provided in this book as such. Readers should always seek the advice of an appropriately qualified person in the reader's home jurisdiction. The Author and Publisher of this book assume no responsibility for information contained in this book and disclaim all liability in respect of such information. In addition, none of the content of this book will form any part of any contract or constitute an offer of any kind.

Any links to third party websites are provided solely for the purpose of your convenience. Links made to websites are made at your own risk and the Author and Publisher accept no liability for any linked sites. When you access a website please understand that it is independent from the Author and Publisher and the Author and Publisher have no control over the content of that website.

Further, a link contained in this book does not mean that the Author or Publisher endorses or accepts any responsibility for the content or the use of such website.

The Author and Publisher do not give any representation regarding the quality, safety, suitability or reliability of any of them or any of the material contained within them. Users must take their own precautions to ensure that what is selected for use is free of such items as viruses, worms, trojan horses and other items of a destructive nature.

All websites, products and services are mentioned, without warranty of any kind, either express or implied, including, but not limited to, the implied warranties of merchant ability and fitness for a particular purpose.

Table of Contents

Disclaimer: 4
Table of Contents 7
Introduction..9
Chapter 1. Finding Time To Write Every Day 13
Chapter 2. Choose 12 Books to Write........................18
Chapter 3. Publish to Profit 24
Chapter 4. Marketing 28
Chapter 5. Time To Start Writing................................32
Chapter 6. Stay Professional 35
Chapter 7. Invest in Your Craft....................................38
Bonus Book - The One Month Author

Introduction.

Welcome to this brand new Writing Challenge designed to help you write and publish 12 books and/or eBooks in one year, and make sales.

Now this might sound like an overly ambitious plan because, after all, 12 books in a year means writing one every month.

Well let's look at it like this:

Is it ambitious?

Yes.

Is it possible?

Absolutely.

Naturally, if you're planning to write and publish a book a month, you're not going to be writing huge tomes of 1,000 pages or more. There's nothing to stop you doing that, but it would mean having more than 24 hours in a day to write. Instead, you'll be looking at writing more modest books with much lower page counts. And let's face it, not many people want to read 1,000 pages. The books you choose to write are entirely up to you, fiction or non-fiction, and I will be walking you through choosing what to write and finding ideas.

Why Write 12 Books in 12 Months?

Well, why not? And don't think about "trying" to write 12 books in 12 months. You ARE going to write them. You're also going to publish them too. And to ensure you make sales, I'm going to show you how to do free online marketing too.

How Long Will All This Planning Take?

I can't tell you how long it will take you to set out your writing plan because that depends entirely on you and how much time you have. It may take you only a couple of days, but it may be a couple of weeks.

Doing a plan for a whole year takes time because you want to make sure you include everything. But it will be fun and it will be great exercise for the creative side of your brain.

What Will I Be Doing?

You're going to plan 12 books/eBooks that you'll be writing over the next 12 months. This means brainstorming ideas, which we're going to look at in more detail.

You're also going to expand these ideas into 12 book outlines. This is going to make the writing so easy to do, and fun. Having an outline means that no matter how much time has passed, all your ideas are still there, outlined in full detail so you'll never forget anything.

You're also going to create a 10-point marketing plan for all your books. This means that every time you publish a book, you go through your 10 marketing steps. Easy.

With a book writing and marketing plan like this, it takes the difficulty out of knowing what to do and when to do it.

How Hard Will This Be?

One of the easiest things in all areas of life is being organised, because you know where everything is, you know what you have to do and when to do it.

And it works for writing too. Having a plan means you know exactly what and when to do everything. Once your plan is set out, you just work your way through it step-by-step.

The hardest part is making the plan because it means finding ideas, turning them into book outlines, and then deciding what else needs to be done (proofing, publishing, marketing, etc.) and in what order.

Planning is the most brain-taxing part of what you'll be doing, but it also takes the shortest time of everything you'll be doing over the next 12 months.

And it makes everything else so much easier.

Will I Keep It Up All Year?

You'll commit to your plan and stick to it if you're determined to do it. If you're not serious about doing this challenge, then you won't do it. But that applies to anything in life. You're either a doer or a quitter, and I can't help you with that.

You could, if you wanted to, make a 12 month plan, and commit to seeing it through for at least 3 months. That way it won't seem as hard as 12 months so you'll feel less intimidated.

Hopefully, by the end of the 3 months, you'll realise that you've already achieved so much that you'll want to keep going. If not, at least you'll have written and published 3 books. And a quitter is always going to be a quitter.

The question isn't WILL you do it for 12 months.

You already know if you will. And if you have to ask, then I already know you won't.

How Much Can I Earn?

I don't know how much money you'll earn from your books, but I know that you can earn as much as you want. Whether you will or not, I have no idea. It all depends on a myriad of factors, including how good your books are, if you market them correctly, what price they are, and plenty of other things besides.

But if you work your plan for the full 12 months then I can't see any reason why you wouldn't make sales, especially with an effective 10-point marketing plan that you use for each one.

How much money you earn is entirely up to you and your books. But what you do in the next 12 months can go on earning you a passive income for years.

All you need right now is the desire to take the 12 Month Writing Challenge, and the commitment to see it through.

In 12 months time, you'll have 12 novels or non-fiction books (or a mixture of both) written and published. Not only that, but because you'll have been working through your marketing plan as well, you'll be making sales. And the great thing about books is that they can go on earning you passive income for years.

There are many authors who write a book a month, and they were all extremely prolific writers which is something you need to strive to be too.

Stephen King wrote The Running Man is a week. He also says he writes 2,000 words in a day, every day, even holidays and weekends. That's 60,000 words a month every month.

Anne Rice wrote Interview With a Vampire in 5 weeks and it's 338 pages long.

Dean Wesley Smith wrote 763 thousand words in one year. Robert Louis Stevenson wrote Dr Jeckle and Mr Hyde in 3 days.

Arthur Conan Doyle wrote his first Sherlock Holmes book in 3 weeks.

Isaac Asimov wrote 400 books during his writing career.

Rachel Aaron was writing 2,000 words a day, but increased it to 10,000 after better planning and even wrote a book, <u>2k to 10k: Writing Faster, Writing Better, and Writing More of What You Love</u>, about how she did it.

Old pulp fiction writers like Earl Stanley Gardner and WT Ballard averaged one million words a year, which is equivalent of 15 full-length novels every single year.

So you can see that writing a book a month for a year is possible with the right planning.

And it all starts now.

Chapter 1.

Finding Time To Write Every Day

Now this is where you begin your 12 month writing plan and it all starts with knowing what and when you're going to be writing every day.

No doubt you're already aware of your hourly writing speed and how many hours you can write in a day, but for this 12 month challenge you need to know more.

You need to be able to divide up your time on a daily basis so that you know how much time you need to do other things and how much time you can use for your writing.

Being able to dedicate as much time as you can to your writing every day will feel great especially knowing that you can use your plan to sit down and write thousands of words every day. Like we discussed in the introduction, Stephen King writes 2,000 words a day, and Rachel Aaron increased her words from 2,000 to 10,000 with better planning. No doubt you can increase your daily word count with practice too.

I know myself that whenever I achieve my daily writing goals, or exceed them, it gives me the most amazing feeling of accomplishment, and also motivates me to write even more.

So now it's time to get out pen and paper and make a list of everything you do in a day/week. It's important to include every single thing and not leave anything out, so include things like shopping, sleeping, eating, personal hygiene, Social Media and TV watching.

This is a list for your eyes only so don't feel too embarrassed to put something on your list. If it's something that takes up time, then it needs to be there.

I once had to do this as an experiment in college. It was to see how much free time we had for studying and doing our assignments. What surprised us all was not only how much free time we had, but how much time we wasted on things that not only were a waste of time, but actually detracted from our lives.

For many people, they were shocked at how much time they wasted in cafes. It seemed that everywhere they went, it involved a stop at a café. Not only were they wasting up to 10 hours a week this way, but the financial cost shocked them too.

In this experiment we also had to look for ways to save time, like batching things we had to do (don't make a separate trip to the post office, go on the way to the supermarket) and cutting out big time wasters, which for me was quitting having long chats whenever I ran into someone, which happened a lot in the town where I lived at the time.

Being more organized was also a huge time saver. I just made a to-do list for every day (just in my head, not written down) and then I'd see it through no matter what, even if I was still busy long after dark.

Getting so much more done every day not only improved my life, but it made me feel so great to be able to get so much done every day. It's a habit I've kept up ever since.

And this is also what you're going to do to make sure you have time to write a book a month for the next year.

Make a list of everything that fills your days.

Then write down next to each one how much time it takes. Don't be measly with your times. Think about each item carefully and how long it actually takes you to do it, not how much time you'd like it to ideally take.

Your list should include everything you do in a week, and how many times a week you do each thing.

Next, add up all the times for the week.

There are 169 hours in a week so your list should add up to less than this.

You now know how much time you have left every week for writing challenges.

If it gives you more time than you need, that's great. If not, then you need to purge your list and get rid of things that you don't need to do and that are a waste of time. Social media is something that you can cut back or cut out. And if you watch soap operas, don't.

Somethings can't be changed (and shouldn't be) like working your day job if you have one and family obligations.

Look at how much time you can comfortably dedicate to your writing challenge every week for the next 12 months, then up it by 10% because you need to feel at least a little pressure.

If you're not sure of your word count, take a couple of weeks to write as many words as you can to see what your weekly rate is. You also need to practice without your inner editor inhibiting you. You need to write fast and write hard which is how the pulp writers used to earn a living because they were paid by word count, not by ongoing royalties so they had to write fast and hard to earn a living.

Every year, writers take part in NaNoWriMo, National Novel Writing Month, where they commit to writing a 50,000-word book beginning 1st November and finishing by 30th November.

Many make it, some don't, and some have gone on to be successful authors after completing the NaNoWriMo challenge and realizing how much writing they can do in a month. Some authors have had their books published that they actually wrote during the challenge, which shows that writing quickly doesn't mean writing badly.

Quite the opposite. I find that the faster I write, the better I write because it doesn't allow time for my inner-critic to interfere or allow me to second-guess myself.

So look at the time you have available to write every week and how much you can write during that time. Adjust your schedule to free up more time if needed. Only you know what you are capable of. But this is a writing challenge, not a writing stroll, so you'll need to push yourself to see it through to the end. It's one thing to write a book in a month, it's another to do it 12 times in a year.

This is why you need to work out your writing times every day of the week so that you can make sure you prioritise those hours for writing and stick to it no matter what.

It doesn't need to be the exact same time every day but you need to know which hours on each day have been put aside exclusively for writing. You also need to train others not to interrupt you during your writing hours, and don't interrupt yourself either by checking emails, social media or text messages. Mute your phone while you write. I have a separate computer for writing and it's all I use it for. I can't check my emails or log into social media on it. And because I've only ever used it for writing, it puts me in the mood to write because as soon as I open it and see the different wallpaper and lack of apps, my mind instantly switches to writing mode. It's like a habitual cue.

If you need more help with finding more time to write, there's a book/eBook that I can definitely recommend. It's called "How To Have a 48 Hour Day" by Don Aslett. I own a digital copy of it and I've read it many times. The author is the master of getting things done and he squeezes more hours into a day than anyone I know. This book is also an incredibly entertaining read, which is why I can't stop reading it, that and it's the most informative book on productivity that I've ever come across. It's all told through the author's life and how he accomplishes so much. He has a refreshingly different take on work and leisure. He says that just because we label something as 'work' it doesn't mean it's hard or not enjoyable. Likewise, just because we label things 'leisure' doesn't mean they're easy or not difficult. Which explains why days out and vacations can be mentally and physically exhausting.

As an example of his work ethic, in one chapter he talks about how he went to stay at his holiday house for 3 months and during that time he built a fence, laid concrete steps, cut back 100 feet of what he called 'the jungle'(he has a lot of land), planted trees and wrote 4 books.

Reading about someone who is such a high achiever and it never tires him, is inspiring and it shows just how much is possible for any of us.

And all it takes is a plan and the commitment to see it through.

When you have your list completed and have your writing times set, then it's time to decide which books you're going to write.

Chapter 2.

Choose 12 Books to Write

This is my most favourite part of writing a book. I love choosing a topic or a story and fleshing it out into a whole outline. Even looking for ideas is fun too because it really gets the creative part of my brain working. If you've written books before, you'll know what I mean.

And the ideas for your books are exclusively yours. No one else has the same idea, it's yours alone. Even if they have a similar idea, they won't work it the way you can.

When I read a book written by someone else, I sometimes think what a great idea it was for a topic or what an amazing story it was that they weaved into an entertaining novel.

To see what I mean, just think about the novel (and subsequent movie) 'The Silence of The Lambs'. If you haven't seen it or read it, then this will be a spoiler alert. It's about a psychiatrist who is also a cannibal and is in a maximum-security asylum from where he assists the FBI in capturing a serial killer. But while giving assistance, he escapes, evades capture and eats the warden who'd tormented him throughout his whole imprisonment.

That story is gold, isn't it? I don't think I could ever come up with a plot as ambitious as that.

But maybe one day....

In the meantime, to write and publish 12 books in a year will be a huge feat.

You need to capture all your ideas upfront so that they are fresh and your mind is motivated. Once they're all written down and you have a detailed outline for each book then you can relax and begin writing your first book safe in the knowledge that every time you finish one book and begin the next, no matter how much time has gone by, your ideas are still there, all organised so that all you have to do is read through them and start writing.

Doing all the planning first frees you up to write all your books, one after the other, knowing that all your ideas are waiting and all the publishing and marketing processes are in place, so all you have to do is work your plan.

What you need to do now is come up with 12 ideas for 12 books. You can publish them as print books or eBooks or both. A few of my books are exclusively eBooks, while others are both. Years ago it used to be a lot harder to publish print books but print on demand technology means anyone can publish a print book.

Sometimes, if your book is only short, say about 15k to 25k words, it may be better to only publish it as an eBook. But we'll discuss this later.

For now, we're only looking for ideas for your books. You may want to write fiction or non-fiction or both. Some authors use different pen names for their fiction and non-fiction books because readers often like to buy books by the same author, so they like to use one name for one subject or fiction series.

There are also authors who write exclusively non-fiction books and will use different pen names if they write on multiple subjects, again to get a following of readers for each author name.

Fiction writers also do the same if they write in different genres.

And of course there are a few authors who write lots of different books on lots of different subjects and they do it all under they're own name. They're so busy writing that they don't worry about readers following them, and yet their books are always popular. I guess most readers think a good book is a good book regardless of who wrote it.

I'm a bit both ways in that regards. When it comes to reading, I have authors whose books I like and I'm always interested if I see a book they've written. On the other hand, I have a lot of books written by authors I've never heard of and I think some of them are indie authors. But I don't care who wrote it if I like the book.

So what do you want to write?

Choose carefully. Don't choose a genre or a subject just because you think its popular and you'll earn more money.

You're going to be doing a lot of writing so you need to choose something you love to write about. Something that you know a lot about or stories you like to tell. You need to be really interested in what you write about otherwise you'll get bored and it will show in your writing.

Years ago, I corresponded with a writer from India, a man who wanted to write romance novels. I asked why he chose that because it's a genre usually written by women. He said it was because he'd done his research and that more romance novels sold more than any other genre. He said romance readers were avid readers and would read 4 or more books a month. He had even enrolled in a romance writing course.

He was absolutely correct that romance outsells all other genres, but he never once said that he wanted to write romance novels. He was only chasing the money.

I lost touch with him after a few months but the last I heard he was not enjoying his course and was finding writing romance a lot harder than he thought. He was even struggling getting to grips with how many sub-genres there are to romance and even sub-sub-genres.

I couldn't help but think he would have been better off writing something he understood and enjoyed.

This is why I can't help with your choices. It's purely a personal preference.

If you don't have any ideas of what you want to write about just start looking. I find that when I look for writing ideas, I quickly go from no idea to idea overload.

You can start by browsing online book stores like Amazon. There are millions of books there, and people that go to Amazon are looking for books to buy. They are buyers so all the books there are written for buyers. Authors who have a lot of books there know what buyers are looking for. This makes it a great place to browse for ideas of your own.

Look at a few book titles and scan the Table of Contents and the blurb. Browse the book categories and see which ones grab your interest. It's possible (and probable) that books you like to read are also the ones you want to write.

Do an online search for blogs on subjects you're interested in and on social media too. This will give you an idea of what people are currently looking for. Maybe they're asking about something that you could write a book about.

You can also browse physical book stores, libraries, newsagents and even DVD stores. I find that airport book stores and newsagents always have a huge range of everything. Looking at magazines can spark ideas too.

If you need more help, I have a book called "Writers Block" that shows you how and where to quickly find ideas for any writing you want to do. You can download a copy right now at https://ruthiswriting.com/books/wb.html.

Every time you think of an idea, write it down immediately. Even if you're not sure if you can use it or not, write it down anyway. It must have piqued your interest for some reason so don't lose it.

Once you have plenty of ideas, decide on the ones you want to use. If you're anything like me, it will be a tough decision because you'll have so many ideas it will be hard to whittle it down to only those that you need now.

When you've thinned your list down to the chosen 12, it's time to work on these.

The ideas you've rejected for now, keep them stored safely in a notebook or computer document, along with as many notes about how you were going to use them. I have a notebook called "Books to Write" full of all my ideas along with a description and explanation on what I was planning to write. I'm always adding to the list because I never want to lose an idea.

Put your 12 ideas in the order you want to write them. This is important, especially if you're writing a series of books. Even if you're not, you need to know the order in which you want to write them.

Next take the first book you want to write and start to flesh it out. Expand each sentence into a paragraph, and then into a page.

Decide on your chapter numbers and what each chapter will contain.

If it's a non-fiction book, for each chapter, write down 10-15 topics you're going to cover.

For fiction, write down the series of events and the scenes in each chapter. This is all explained in detail in "The One Month Author", the free bonus eBook you received.

For each topic in each chapter, write 3 sub-topics you're going to cover.

Do the same for the fiction chapters. 3 things that will happen in each event and scene.

This is your book outline. In "The One Month Author" it explains in full how to outline your book and then turn it into a blueprint, which contains everything you need to write your book. You simply follow the blueprint and your book will be written. It streamlines the whole writing process, making it easy to write a book a month, because your creative mind will be free to write without having to worry about what comes next or how to write something.

Of course, outlines and blueprints are only guides. Deviate when great ideas come up on the fly. Don't stick rigidly to an outline or blueprint if you think of better things along the way.

Plan all your book outlines and blueprints the same way until you have them all completed and ready for you to start writing.

One of the best things about planning books in such detail is that no matter how far along you are in your 12 month plan, you can just pick up the next outline/blueprint and start writing.

12 months is a long time to consistently work through a plan, and if you didn't have your books outlined and ready to write, you'd get weary of starting so many books from scratch. But this way, they're ready and just waiting to be written, with no effort needed.

Can you imagine how easy it would be if every time you wanted to write a book someone just handed you a complete book blueprint so all you had to do was sit down and write it?

Well that's what it will feel like. As time goes on over the next 12 months, you'll forget what books are in your list or what you put in your outlines. So every month you'll open a new blueprint and see it with "fresh" eyes.

I'm betting you'll be impressed with how good all the ideas are. It always feels that way when I haven't read my own writing for a while.

And with your 12 blueprints ready, it's time to plan your publishing schedule.

Chapter 3.

Publish to Profit

The time to publish each book is as soon as you've finished writing it, or you could have a regular publishing schedule and use the same date each month. For instance, you could publish all your books on the last day of the month they were written.

But there's a few things you need to do first.

Your manuscript needs the prelim pages adding at the front. These usually include a copyright page, a dedication page, a disclaimer page and a Table of Contents. If you want to publish a print book, you may need to add in a blank page to make sure that your first chapter begins on the right hand page, known in the publishing business as the recto page, which is the side where all books begin, eBooks, on the other hand, don't have recto and verso pages, nor page numbers.

You can choose to have whatever pages you want or that your book needs. For instance, novels don't usually have a Table of Contents or a disclaimer page. You can also have a page listing your other books. You can also put some of these pages at the back if you prefer. Looking at similar books to yours can give you ideas.

Another thing your book needs is a cover. There are companies that make covers and there's online software you can use as well as software you can buy.

It's also possible to create your own flat cover as a text document with a coloured background and save it as an image. A print book will need a spine and back cover too and a barcode, but book cover creating software takes care of all that.

But before you start writing your books, you need to decide how and where to get your book covers from. If you decide to only publish your books through Amazon's KDP platform, they provide free cover creating software. Many authors only publish their books through Amazon for speed and simplicity.

Doing this though, limits your books to being only available from one store.

There's a Company called Smashwords who only publish eBooks, but if that's the only way you want to publish them, Smashwords provides worldwide distribution. Both Amazon and Smashwords are free to use, but they do keep a small percentage of your book sales.

If you prefer to pay for a whole publishing package, there are publishers like Booklocker or Bookbaby, who will do all the publishing process for you, but charge a few hundred dollars for the service.

Publishing Companies like these do make it effortless to publish your books, but you'll need to sell a lot of copies just to recoup your cost and break even.

You could, if you wanted to, send your manuscripts to traditional publishing companies. But many of these companies are wary of first-time authors and prefer only receiving manuscripts from agents.

There are many publishing companies accepting unsolicited manuscripts, but you'd have to find those that are looking for books in your genre or the subject you've written about. They are choosy about what they're looking for.

For instance, Harlequin only publish romance novels. They have never published anything else. But even with a one-genre company like this, they have dozens of sub-genres and are extremely specific about the types of stories they'll accept. So it can take a lot of research to find the right publishing company for your books, unless of course, you choose the company first and write specifically for them.

But using a traditional publishing company will only hinder your goal of having 12 books written and published in a year, so you need to know how to publish your books yourself.

As I previously said, using Amazon exclusively is fast and simple. Or you can sign up for an account with Ingram Sparks who charge a small fee for publishing, but they do make your books available worldwide and provide book cover software. They also make your books available to libraries.

Your books also need an ISBN, an International Standard Book Number. These are the 13-digit numbers that you see on the barcode.

Book stores won't stock books without a barcode. If you publish your books on Amazon without an ISBN, Amazon lists themselves as the publisher. It looks so much more professional with your own ISBN. So if you publish a book as an eBook and print book, each will need a separate ISBN. Ditto for hard back and paper back.

Each country has it's own company that sells ISBNs. In the US it's a company called Bowker. ISBNs are cheaper if you by them in blocks rather than individually, and as you're going to need a dozen or two, you need to buy them upfront.

Once you have your ISBNs, every time you publish a book, you assign one of the numbers to it, and then update your ISBN account to register it.

There may be other rules to book publishing depending on the country you live in, so you'll need to search online to find this information. The ISBN company should have it.

So to summarise what you need to do in advance to publish your books, is have your prelim pages ready so that you can quickly add a copyright page or a disclaimer page without having to write them every time.

Decide where you're going to get your book covers from, or get them upfront so they're ready.

Buy your ISBN's so you can quickly assign and register them to each book before you publish them.

Set up an account with the company you're going to use to publish your books, and make sure you're aware of the publishing process that they use and that you're clear on what you have to do to publish each book, so that you don't waste time later.

Naturally, each time you publish a book it will be easier and faster then the last time because you'll know what you're doing.

When I first started publishing my own books years ago, it was a lot harder and it took me a while to figure out how to do it all.

There were no eBooks or amazon publishing back then. Novels all had to be published as print books and non-fiction could only be unsecured PDF downloads, so the problem of online copyright theft was huge. My work was always getting stolen online, and I even had to hire lawyers in other countries to sort it out.

But now eBooks are harder to steal, and POD is widely available.

If you want to simplify the whole publishing process for now, you can simply forget about buying ISBN's and publish your books through kdp.amazon.com. It's fast and free to set up an account, they provide free and simple cover creating software which comes with free images if you need them, and it's one-click easy to upload your manuscript which is then automatically formatted for you and made available worldwide.

But like I said, although it's easy, it does limit you to only one bookstore selling your books. You could do it this way for now and change your mind later.

The choice is entirely up to you.

Chapter 4.

Marketing

So now you've planned and outlined all your books and you know how you're going to publish them.

Now comes the most important part. Marketing. Without the correct marketing, your book sales won't be great. They may not even exist at all.

And just like how you've set up your book outlines and your publishing, your marketing needs to be set up in advance too. You need to know exactly what you're going to do to let everyone know that your books are there and how great they are, before you write and publish them.

Thankfully, book marketing is so much easier than it used to be. Years ago, authors spent a fortune on advertisements in magazines and newspapers, and had to spend weeks and months doing book tours.

But now you can harness the global reach of the internet to market your book all over the world.

No doubt you already have your own blog or website and a list of subscribers, which means you're already ahead of the marketing game. Your site visitors and subscribers are already interested in you and what you have to offer so you can pre-market your books to them by telling them how great the book is that you're writing and how much they'll love it when it's published soon.

Pre-marketing like this is also great for helping you to stick to your monthly writing and publishing schedule when you already have readers waiting to buy a copy. You could also publish it at an introductory discounted price to entice early sales.

If you have a social media account and online followers, this is also a great place to announce each book. Only use accounts that are for you as a writer, not an account that you use for keeping in touch with family and friends.

I have an account on twitter that I use to connect with other writers, and I use it to talk about my books and my blogs. It's the perfect place for marketing. I also have a LinkedIn account for the same purpose.

There are plenty of social media sites online, but don't sign up to too many because it can get confusing to what you posted and when. It can also become too time consuming to keep up with it all.

Using a calendar or diary can help you keep up with marketing. You can fill it in every time you want to upload something. So if you decide to publish blog posts on Mondays and Wednesdays, you can write it in your calendar or in your diary so that you don't forget.

Giving away the first chapter of your books for free can be good as a marketing tool too, as long as it contains a link at the end to where they can buy a copy. To do this, the first chapter of your book needs to be extremely intriguing and end on a hook that makes the reader disappointed that they don't know what happens next and will have to buy a copy to find out.

You can also use other people's blogs for marketing too. Leaving comments can be helpful if you do it subtly. Don't blatantly talk about your book, but perhaps mention that you wrote one and hopefully people will be curious enough to click on your profile link to find out more. Or don't even mention your book at all, just leave on incredibly useful and insightful comment so that others will want to know more about you.

If you can find a blog that accepts guest posts, do that. Write an article that relates to your book's topic. Guest posts usually include a link to the author's website or blog so if they like your article they can find out more about you.

The blog you choose for guest posting needs to be extremely relevant to what your books are about. Even if you've written fiction, you can look for a blog or website where the owner writes in the same genre as you, or they are someone who is interested in the same genre. Then write an article about it or write a short story. Anything that gets people interested to know more is fine.

You can also send a copy of your manuscript to a book review site. Make sure yours is the type of book they're interested in and that they are currently accepting manuscripts. The downside is that most of these sites are so busy that it can be weeks before they get around to reviewing your book which won't help you now but can be a big help in the future.

Article directories can also be used for marketing. Some of them, such as Medium, have programs set up so that writers get paid. You can upload articles or stories and the more they get read, the more you can earn, plus you can include links to your books or your blog or website, or wherever they can find your books.

As I said at the beginning, marketing is crucial, but it doesn't have to be hard, and it doesn't have to cost anything. Giving away free first chapters is fast and so is sending a copy of your manuscript to a book review site. And if you write a guest post or an article/story for an online directory, you can earn money too.

But you need to know how you're going to market each of your books. Different subjects and different genres need marketing in different places.

Devise a 10-point marketing plan for each of your books that includes 10 different places you're going to use. Write down the exact sites you'll be using. You can even write the guest posts or directory articles/stories now so that you don't have to waste time later or in case you get a bit behind schedule and don't have time. You already have the detailed blueprints of all your books, so you already know everything they're going to contain. You can use this for ideas for your marketing.

Once you've listed your 10-point marketing plan for each book, when you've finished writing a book and published it, all you have to do is work your way through your plan. Go to each site in your list and make a post, a comment or upload an article/story. You can make adjustments to your marketing plan as you go along, if you get better ideas, but most of the work will have been done, so it won't take long to finish it.

The most important place to market your books is on your own blog or website. You can even set up the sales pages in advance and write "coming soon".

Your sales page should talk about how great the book is and most importantly, how it will benefit the reader.

If your book is non-fiction, you can include a bullet list of everything the reader is going to learn.

If it's a fiction book, you can fill the sales page with a curiosity-driven overview of the story, plus the emotion the reader will feel.

Part of the sales page content can also be used for the back-cover blurb of your book. Or likewise, the back cover blurb of your book can be included in your sales page.

Again, having these pages set up ahead of time will be a real time-saver later. You can make a few changes to it later if you want, but most of it will be fine and all you have to add is a small image of the book cover and a link to where they can buy it online.

When you publish a book, you also have to include a blurb that you upload at the same time as your manuscript. The information on your sales page can be used for this too.

And once you have your 10-point marketing plan for each book and your marketing content written out and ready to upload, all the pre-work is done.

It's time to get down to writing your books.

Let the fun begin.

Chapter 5.

Time To Start Writing

So now you have everything ready in advance, and all that you need to do now is start writing. Working on a new book is always exciting and now you have 12 to write, and they are already outlined in detail and just begging to be written.

The way that I like to work is that, when I write a book, I prefer to do that and nothing else. Sometimes, if I get a bit bored or I feel that I need a break, I'll work on a few marketing articles or blog posts, and then get straight back to my book.

I usually batch write my social media and blog posts and schedule them to be automatically published at later dates. I do the same with emails and marketing articles too. That way my online presence is taking care of itself leaving me free to focus on my book writing.

Of course, there are times when I differ how I work and I'll spend hours writing my book and then end the day blogging and writing articles.

I guess it all depends on how I feel at the time. Mostly though, I batch smaller writing projects.

But when it comes to book writing, one thing is certain, I like to write for as long as I can and get into the flow state. This means my focus is 100% on what I'm doing and I'm able to block out everything else. Not only is this great for productivity, but it's also incredibly therapeutic to be able to tune out the rest of the world for a while.

Another thing I find, and I'm not sure if it's just me or if it happens to everyone, if I don't stick at something, I get bored with it and can't focus anymore. This is why it's important for me to get my book written and to work on it every day because once I lose track of what I'm doing, I can sometimes lose interest too.

This is why whatever I write about, whether it's fiction or non-fiction, it has to be something I'm interested in, otherwise I lose interest fast.

So my advice is to write as much as you can as often as you can and don't miss a day. There's time in every day to get some writing done, even if you only have an hour, or you have to give up some TV watching time or go to bed a bit later.

When I'm working on a large writing project, like a book, I like to binge write every day for as long as I can, with hour after hour of head-down non-stop writing.

If I'm writing non-fiction, I often also write a short report based on the subject of my book that I can give away to use as free marketing. I usually allow others to give it away too.

I simply jot down ideas for the report as I write my book, or else I write the report as one big outline of what the book is about.

These short reports can be written in a couple of hours and are a great marketing tool. I've written all about how to write a short report or eBook as a bonus chapter in the 7-day eBook Writing and Publishing System https://ruthiswriting.com/books/7day.html.

But right now it's time to open your first outline/blueprint and begin writing your first book.

During your year of writing, you'll probably come up with even more book writing ideas. This happens to me all the time. I find that the best thing to do is write the ideas down in as much detail as you can (which probably won't be much at this stage) and then forget about it and get back to writing, secure in the knowledge that your idea is safe.

My crazy monkey mind gets bombarded with ideas all the time, so I have one notebook where I quickly write down all my book ideas as they come to me. I also have another one where I write down all my blog and article ideas as soon as arrive. Working this way means I never lose a brilliant idea, I know exactly where to find it, and it frees up my mind so that I can carry on writing.

Not only is capturing ideas quickly helpful for keeping me focused but reading through them later is inspiring and it gets the ideas flowing freely again.

The same thing will happen with your 12 Month Writing Plan. As time goes by, you'll forget the other books you're going to write, but because you have such detailed blueprints of all your ideas, plus a complete plan of what to write and when to write it, you'll have no trouble writing the next book.

Plus, when you re-read your plans and outlines with "fresh" eyes, it will inspire you and get you in the writing mood immediately.

You'll be so glad you have such detailed blueprints to follow because even though it may be months since you wrote it, it's all still there, so you can start writing straight away.

You may find that you might feel a bit unsure of the publishing and marketing process if you've never done it before. If this is the case, try and forget about it for now and glue all your attention to your writing instead.

Things always seem unclear if it's something you've never done before. But things become clear once you do them and work through the process. And because you're going to be doing it 12 times, you'll get to be a pro at it. Every time you do it, it will be easier the next time, and the next.

You have a detailed plan so all you have to do is follow it, and anything you're unsure about will become clear as you go along.

The most important thing right now is to make a start and write your first book. Starting something is always THE most important step.

Remember the words of Martin Luther King Jr "You don't have to see the whole staircase, just take the first step".

Or how about the words of online guru Mike Littman "You don't have to get it right; you just have to get it going."

So head down, start writing. The hardest work is already done.

Chapter 6.

Stay Professional

You may be wondering what being professional has to do with writing books. Well, it has a lot to do with it.

The word professional, in the broad sense, means a person who is paid for what they do. But for this chapter, I mean to act like a mature, intelligent business person.

Imagine that you've already written dozens of books and sold millions of copies, and because of this, you have millions of followers on social media, and people in the media keep contacting you for interviews.

Would you act differently? Of course you would. You'd be careful about what you said online and in interviews, and in public you'd make sure you behaved with integrity in case people recognized you. You wouldn't make snarky comments on social media or post photos of yourself on boozy nights out with your mates.

And you shouldn't be doing all this now either. You need to be professional at all times so that you'll be respected as a writer. Your writing needs to be professional too. Don't write garbage and expect people to buy it. Bad reviews will kill sales.

There's a saying that how you do anything is how you do everything, and I believe it's true. People are who they are. People aren't sometimes nice and sometimes nasty. They may pretend to be nice sometimes, but it's only pretense.

I was talking about this recently with someone who was telling me that their neighbour seemed like a nice person, but she was cruel to her young child and could be heard screaming at him for hours. She said to me "She's a bad mother." I said, "No. She's a bad person." I told her that people are what they are. A person who is cruel to children or cruel to animals, is a cruel person. If they're greedy with food, they're greedy with everything. If they're lazy at home, they're lazy at work too. They can't be both productive AND lazy.

This is why you need to be professional and above reproach in every area of your life. I make it a personal rule never to write something in an email, or say something to someone in private, that I wouldn't want the whole world to know. Even in my journal, I'm careful about what I write in case it ever gets into the wrong hands. I don't think a burglar would ever steal my journal and read it, but you never know what else may happen.

You can't be a respected author if you drive around with your car windows open, blaring music, or upset your neighbours, get drunk in public or take illegal drugs. You need to behave better than that.

"Fake it till you make it", is what they say, as well as "Act as if it's already happened".

You don't want to become a successful writer and then regret your low-class behaviour in the past. Often, it's the bad behaviour in the past that can jeopardise your success in the future. We see it happen to celebrities all the time. And it only takes one wrong Tweet or one nasty comment online to make people want to never buy your books. Sadly, we are remembered more for the few bad things we've done rather than the million good things.

Also, if you begin to act like a professional writer, soon you'll become one, because we are what we repeatedly do. So start as you mean to go on. If others scoff at your writing (and they will) ignore it and stay professional. Don't react to hurtful criticism. Instead let it fuel you to show them they're wrong.

All writers suffer their fair share (and often more than their fair share) of friends and family ridiculing what they do. But if you're behaving professionally you can let it slide and say nothing, no matter how much it hurts.

It's a sad but true fact of life that those who want to succeed, are pulled down by those who don't. It's like the 'crabs in the bucket' situation, where if one crab gets to the top of the bucket and tries to climb out, the others will reach up and pull it back in. Unfortunately this same thing happens to those with ambition. They get pulled down by those who can't stand to see others rise above them. I've been earning my living as a writer for over 20 years now, and to this day my family refuse to discuss it, and if I bring it up, they quickly change the subject. It's something that I've never understood, but I've had to accept. And none of them have ever done anything but have a mediocre job and a mediocre life.

I'm not saying all this to scare or upset you, and I'm not saying it because it might happen to you. I'm saying it because it WILL happen to you, so you need to be prepared.

Just remember, it's only amateurs who give in when the going gets hard. Professionals accept no excuses and continue writing no matter what.

An amateur loves what they do. A professional also loves what they do, and they love it so much they dedicate their life to it and do it for money.

A professional writer endures adversity, never takes failure personally, and respects their craft.

A professional is also tidy. You cannot create great work if you're disordered and constantly living in chaos. It's said that the muse mustn't soil her gown when she enters, so paths must be swept, and carpets vacuumed.

To be a professional is a decision you make.

Once you see yourself as a professional and start acting like one, you are one.

It's as simple as that.

From this moment on, be the professional you need to be.

Chapter 7.

Invest in Your Craft

Too often I come across writers who are afraid to invest in their craft. They say they want to be a writer and are willing to do anything. But they won't financially invest in it. Instead, they ask "Is there any way to do it for free?"

They'll go to a café and splash $7 for a coffee and cake, but they don't want to invest $7 in a book about writing. They use excuses like "I want to make money, not spend money."

But it's not spending. It's investing.

Any business you want to start takes money. Even a writing business, so you need to invest in the right equipment.

Here's a good example of false economy. I live in an apartment complex, and we have a caretaker who does all the daily and weekly cleaning and maintenance jobs. But he won't buy the equipment he needs and instead buys inferior products, like he has a small domestic vacuum instead of a strong commercial one so it takes longer to vacuum the carpets than it should.

And when there are bigger jobs to do, like pressure washing, we have to get someone else in to do it. It's not that the caretaker doesn't want to do it (on the contrary, he wants to earn the extra money for doing it) but he doesn't have the right equipment. His pressure washer is a cheap one from the local hardware shop so is unsuitable for cleaning large outdoor areas. So, he's constantly losing money because he penny-pinches on his equipment so we can't pay him for large jobs, and he has to pay his cleaner to work longer hours too.

The same is true for being a professional writer, you need the correct tools for the job.

Of course, if you're already writing, you'll have a computer, printer and internet connection.

You don't even need an internet connection all the time. Only if you're researching or uploading. I've known some writers who say they get more done when they don't have constant internet access. Instead, they write at home and then go to the library or café to use the internet. That way they batch all their online jobs which saves time and makes them more productive.

For most people, a computer, printer and internet connection are something they already have anyway, and you probably do too. I have a small, cheap printer and a 13" Mac Book Pro that I use for most of my work. I also have an iPad Air from 2013 that someone gave me when they upgraded to a newer model. I still use it for typing sometimes (It came with an attachable keyboard) which shows that whatever you already have will be suitable for writing.

But it's not just hardware you need. It might be software or a course, a seminar, a class or an eBook.

Whatever it is, if it will help you, buy it. Everything that I've ever bought to do with my writing, as well as being tax deductible, has earned me far more money than it cost to buy it.

And I've invested a lot of money over the last 20+ years, from a $20 eBook all the way up to a $2,000 marketing course. I've bought copious amounts of books and courses on writing, blogging, marketing, copywriting, working online, SEO, self-publishing, web-design, productivity, and much more. I even purchased the full Adobe suite of software which included Photoshop and the mighty Dreamweaver web design software. And it's all paid off.

Don't get me wrong. I don't buy everything I see. I take my time and choose carefully. But I do make sure that I make the most out of all my investments. As an example, the first eBook I bought was about how to write a book in a month (I bought it a long time ago), I worked my way through it and wrote a novel which I then published and sold thousands of copies. As you can imagine, I was elated.

I've also done the same with everything I've bought. When I bought another eBook about how to write a book in 10 days, I worked my way through that too, and viola. I had another published book that's still selling today. And I worked my way through the $2,000 marketing course and used it to sell even more books.

There isn't one thing that I've regretted buying because I always think that even if I only find one gold nugget of information that helps me, then it was worth the price.

So, my advice to you is to do the same and invest in whatever will move your life or your business forward. I even once bought a book called "<u>Is There Life After Housework?</u>' to help me do the cleaning faster so that I have more time to write. And that book is gold. I've read it over and over again because it's such an entertaining read and it has so much useful information like how to clean the bathroom in 3½ minutes. I can't sit down and write until the dishes are done and the house is clean, so I needed that book. And it's helped me to earn money too, as well as making housework easier.

Being organized is crucial to getting more writing done. Despite what most people think, it's easier to be organised than disorganised.

When I get up in the morning, I already know what I'm going to have for breakfast because I've already decided the night before. I get up, get washed and dressed, make the bed, have breakfast, do the dishes, do the housework and then I sit and write.

When I stop for lunch and dinner, I already know what I'm going to have, and I've already got anything I need out of the freezer. Often, I'll prep food for dinner straight after lunch to save time later.

I don't envy people who get up every day and have no clue what they're going to do all day. I have a cleaning schedule, a laundry schedule, and a writing schedule, so I always know what to do and when to do it, which eliminates a lot of decision making or trying to remember the last time I cleaned something.

I'm the same with my writing, I don't finish one day without writing down what I'll be working on the next day. That way, all I have to do is look in my diary and then I can get straight down to writing.

Being organised means I get so much done in a day, plus I have plenty of time for relaxing too.

Being organised and investing in everything you need will help you too, and you'll need it to get a whole lot of writing done in the next year, It will also help you every year after that too.

You have one whole year of writing ahead of you. 12 books to write and publish, and it will be both fun and exhilarating, and the satisfaction you'll feel at the end of it all will make it all feel worthwhile. And don't forget all the book sales.

Not only that, but there'll be plenty of knock-on effects from your 12 months Writing Challenge, including a writing routine that you'll carry on using for years.

And it all starts right here, right now.

Set yourself a writing routine and stick to it. Don't cheat yourself. Use your writing time to actually do your writing. Don't waste it looking at your phone, constantly checking emails.

And likewise, don't cheat yourself on investing in anything you need that will help you achieve your writing goals.

Write out your plan to write your 12 books in the next year, and then stick to your plan for the next 12 months.

Having a detailed plan means that all the big decisions have been made, and decision-making can be the hardest part of all. Once I've made my decisions, it makes the writing easier, because although it takes a long time, my mind is free to write.

Whenever I write a book, the most brain-taxing part is outlining the chapters and putting them in order. Once that's done, writing the manuscript is easy, or at least easy-er. It's the most time-consuming part, but the least brain-straining. It's also the most enjoyable part.

So now it's time for you to stop reading and start planning your own 12 Month Writing Challenge.

If it makes you feel any better, this book that you're reading is the first in my own 12 month writing plan and it only took me one week to write this book, write a short report based on it, and outline my marketing articles and blog posts. So this book and the report will get published at the same time, and the marketing is written and scheduled over the next 2 to 3 weeks.

Which gives me ample time to get started on my next book, so I'm already ahead of schedule.

And with my 12-month writing plan it's easy to keep going because all I have to do is look at what's next on my list.

I hope it all goes smoothly for you too.

You've already made the right investment in your writing career by investing in this book.

So now it's up to you to work your way through it, set up your plan, and then work it over the next 12 months.

Doing this will ensure that your investment will repay you hundreds (and hopefully thousands) of times what it cost you.

It was only a small investment (financially speaking) but it's one that you can use to reap huge rewards.

By this time next year you'll have a dozen books selling all over the world.

How great will that be?

And it all starts with the first book that I hope to see for sale in online bookstores real soon.

Good luck my writing friend.

End.

BONUS BOOK

The One Month Author

THE ONE MONTH AUTHOR

The Monthly Challenge Writing Series

Book 4

Copyright © 2021 by Ruth Barringham

Published in Australia

The author is the copyright owner of this work and no part may be reproduced by any process, nor may any other exclusive right be exercised without the permission of the Author.

This book is sold subject to the condition that it shall not, by way of trade or otherwise, be lent, re-sold, hired out, published electronically online or otherwise circulated without the Author's prior consent. All instances of copyright infringement will be dealt with to the full extent of the law.

The Author is not a lawyer or an accountant and does not intend to render legal, accounting or other professional advice within this book. No guarantees of income, sales or results are promised. It is recommended that users of this book seek legal, accounting and other independent professional business advice before starting any business or acting upon any advice given herein.

ISBN: eBook   978-0-9871151-8-8

Also by Ruth Barringham

How to Quit Smoking

How To Write An Article In 15 Minutes Or Less

Goodbye Writer's Block

7 Day Ebook Writing and Publishing System

Living The Laptop Lifestyle

Mission Critical for Life

The Monthly Challenge Writing Series

Book 1 - Quick Cash Freelance Writing

Book 2 - Build A Lucrative Niche Website

Book 3 - Fast & Profitable Article Writing

Book 4 - The One Month Author

See more of my books on my website

https://ruthiswriting.com

Disclaimer:

The Author and Publisher have used their best efforts in preparing this book. The Author and Publisher make no representation or warranties with respect to the accuracy, applicability, fitness, or completeness of the contents of this book.

The Author is not a lawyer or an accountant and does not intend to render legal, accounting or other professional advice within this book. No guarantees of income, sales or results are promised. It is recommended that users of this book seek legal, accounting and other independent professional business advice before starting any business or acting upon any advice given herein.

The information contained in this book is strictly for information purposes. Therefore, if you wish to apply ideas contained in this book, you are taking full responsibility for your actions. Whilst we hope you find the contents of this book interesting and informative, the contents are for general information purposes only and do not constitute advice. We believe the contents to be true and accurate as at the date of writing but can give no assurances or warranty regarding the accuracy, currency or applicability of any of the contents in relation to specific situations and particular circumstances.

This book is not intended to be a source for advice, and thus the reader should not rely on any information provided in this book as such. Readers should always seek the advice of an appropriately qualified person in the reader's home jurisdiction. The Author and Publisher of this book assume no responsibility for information contained in this book and disclaim all liability in respect of such information. In addition, none of the content of this book will form any part of any contract or constitute an offer of any kind.

Any links to third party websites are provided solely for the purpose of your convenience. Links made to websites are made at your own risk and the Author and Publisher accept no liability for any linked sites. When you access a website please understand that it is independent from the Author and Publisher and the Author and Publisher have no control over the content of that website.

Further, a link contained in this book does not mean that the Author or Publisher endorses or accepts any responsibility for the content or the use of such website.

The Author and Publisher do not give any representation regarding the quality, safety, suitability or reliability of any of them or any of the material contained within them. Users must take their own precautions to ensure that what is selected for use is free of such items as viruses, worms, trojan horses and other items of a destructive nature.

All websites, products and services are mentioned, without warranty of any kind, either express or implied, including, but not limited to, the implied warranties of merchant ability and fitness for a particular purpose.

Table of Contents

The One Month Author 1

Disclaimer: 4

Table of Contents 7

Introduction 9

Chapter 1. Why Write a Book fast? 11

Chapter 2. How To Write a Great Book 14

Chapter 3. What to Avoid – Ignore This at Your Peril 17

Chapter 4. Choosing a Topic 20

Chapter 5. How To Write Quickly 23

Chapter 6. 27The Plot Thickens 27

Chapter 7. Research Fast 31

Chapter 8. Create a Book Outline 35

Chapter 9. 39From Outline To Blueprint To Manuscript. 39

Chapter 10. Creating Characters. 42

Chapter 11. Editing To Perfection 47

Chapter 12. Writing Your Own Life Story 49

Chapter 13. Marketing & Selling Your Book 53

Chapter 14. Writing Wrap Up 59

Introduction.

Hello and welcome to the 4th and final eBook in the Monthly Challenge Writing Series.

All three previous eBooks were about how to earn money from short writing projects.

> Freelance Writing
>
> Niche Websites
>
> Article Writing

In this final eBook we're going to look at earning money from a long writing project which is writing a book manuscript, both fiction and non-fiction. And while this may seem a much bigger writing task, just like the other 3 eBooks, it can be done in a month. And you'll be guided through the whole process.

So all you have to do is work your way through this eBook, and in just a month, you'll have your own manuscript written. We'll also be looking at marketing and selling it too.

But let me begin by congratulating you on taking this massive step on your writing and publishing journey, because starting can be the hardest thing of all. But by buying this eBook, you've already begun. And when you commit to seeing this project through, your investment will repay you with the satisfaction of writing a manuscript, the immense feeling of achievement, and hopefully sales of your book.

So this is the beginning of your 30-day journey from idea to completed manuscript. And it doesn't matter if you want to write fiction or non-fiction because this system of writing that I'm going to show you works for both. And it not only makes it easy to do, but will also allow you to write at unbelievable speeds from idea to outline to completed manuscript.

I'll then walk you through publishing, marketing, and making sales.

All you have to do is work your way through the process and you're guaranteed to have a manuscript finished at the end. The only way you can fail is if you don't do it.

And if you're wondering how you'll be able to write a whole book in a month, don't worry. I've included some writing exercises to show you how fast you can write. Not only will you see how fast, but you'll also see how easy it can be.

So many people think that they can't write a book because it's too hard or it will take too long. But you're about to discover neither of those things are true.

I've been working as a writer and author for over 20 years, and I've written many books and co-authored two books as well. And not one of them took over a month to write.

And now I'm going to show you how you can do it too.

So let's begin.

Chapter 1.

Why Write a Book fast?

You might be wondering what is the big deal about writing a book fast? I look at it this way. Why would you want to write a book slowly?

The most successful authors are those who can write fast.

My co-author on a previous book, Yuwanda Black, is an extremely prolific writer and has written 21 books in a year. That's nearly two books a month. She also is a freelance writer and runs a successful blog. This woman is a writing and publishing machine.

Another co-author of mine Nick Daws, is also the author of "Write Any Book in 28 Days...Or Less" and "The 10-Day eBook." So he knows how to write fast.

One of the techniques of writing quickly is to use **WAYS** which stands for Write As You Speak. It works because we are more clear in what we're saying when we speak because we don't stop and second-guess ourselves or edit what we're saying. So writing the same way is fast.

Some writers earn their money writing non-fiction with articles, stories and other works, while at the same time they long to write a novel but think it will take too long so they think they don't have the time.

But the writing process in this book will allow you to do both because it applies to fiction as well as non-fiction, and the speed it allows you to write at, means you'll have the time to write as much as you want.

The process is a simple one – from idea, to outline, to blueprint, to manuscript.

And don't worry if you don't know what you want to write about because we'll be going through that too. You'll go from trying to find just one idea, to idea overload.

And once you have your idea, we'll go through how to expand it into an outline fast. That way you won't forget a thing.

You may be thinking that all this speed might negatively impact what you're doing.

But there is no relationship between the time it takes you to write something and the quality and value of what you've written.

Readers judge a book by the results they get from reading it, or the enjoyment and emotional value they get from a fiction book. They really don't care whether it took you a month to write it or a year.

I recently read a book about how to write a book in a week, and the book itself was written in a week and the author explained how he did it, which is what the book was about. I found it fascinating and not once did I think it was garbage just because he wrote it quickly. It was highly entertaining to read about his process.

If you can write a book in a month, it means you can write 12 books in a year. Can you imagine how great that would be if in a year's time you were the author of 12 books?

To produce books this fast means you shouldn't get hung up on perfection. Any author will tell you that they never think a book they've written is perfect and years later, if they read it again, they'll still find things they want to change, even if it's a best seller.

Instead its important to aim for your book to be 'good enough' because no matter what you do it will never seem to be perfect, which it's probably because there's no such thing.

But when you follow the process of outlining, blueprinting and writing a book fast it's not only easy to do, it's repeatable. So once you've done it, you can do it again and again. And because it's easy, it's also fun. But don't get me wrong. It's still work. The only difference is that it's not hard. The One Month Author System walks you through the whole process.

All you have to do is commit to seeing it through with self-discipline and motivation.

Just remember the saying – discipline weighs ounces, while regret weighs tons.

Chapter 2.

How To Write a Great Book

There are several reasons why people decide they want to write a book including:

- Money

- To Help People

- For the Enjoyment of Writing

- To Work From Home

These are all excellent reasons and each of them will give you a great feeling of accomplishment when you're holding your manuscript in your hand (or seeing it on your computer).

And it's this feeling that motivates you to want to do it. It will also get rid of the regret of never doing it.

And now you have what it takes because you already have your own motivation, and this eBook that will lead you through everything you need to do to get your book written.

So let's get started.

The first thing you need is a place to write. This can be anywhere at home, or in a café, or at the library.

Children's author, Jacqueline Wilson, only writes on the train when she's travelling. She finds it to be the perfect time because it's otherwise wasted time, and the perfect place because there are no interruptions. Likewise, novelist Rachel Aaron, goes to a local café to write because no one interrupts her and she finds she can write faster there. She is also the author of "2,000 to 10,000" which is all about how she increased her daily writing output from 2k words a day to 10k.

You also need to choose the best time to write. This might be constrained because of work and family commitments, or if you're free to choose your own time, you can figure out whether you're a morning, afternoon or evening writer. I always like to have a time that I write every day otherwise I'm always wondering when I'll get it done. I sit and write at different times on different day, but it's still a schedule. Horror author, Stephen King, says you should get a writing schedule and stick to it. It's ok to write more, but never write less.

At first it might be hard to choose a time to write, but it won't take long to figure out what works best for you, once you start writing regularly.

And this is where to start. Right here.

Now remember, this writing project has a deadline – one month. But this isn't a bad thing. Just like when you were at school and given an assignment to complete in an allotted time, a deadline will make you more productive.

And the process you're about to learn will show you just how productive you can be because using an outline makes you write faster (200-300 words in 5 minutes) plus it helps with focus and concentration.

Having an outline also means that whenever you stop writing, it's easy to pick up again from where you left off, even if it's been a few days.

But you won't want to stop writing once you start. Sometimes though, starting can be the hardest thing. But don't worry because this writing method makes it easy. It's just like cooking. You find a recipe, follow the instructions, and viola, you have a finished dish. It's the same way with writing. You follow the instructions in this eBook, and viola. You have a finished manuscript.

Repeating the process is easy too.

If you want to write several books, start your next book straight away to keep the writing momentum going. Don't wait for sales from your first book. Just keep writing.

There are writers who write 12 books a year, some even write more, and if you want to join them, writing must be your priority.

If you're wondering where you'll find the time to write, you'll always find the time to write, or you'll always find excuses not to write, and do nothing.

It's up to you.

But you've come this far so keep going.

Chapter 3.

What to Avoid – Ignore This at Your Peril

The most important thing for you right now, is that you need to get your book written. You may have promised yourself before (and you may have promised yourself several times in the past) that you were going to write a book. But this time you're actually going to do it. No excuses. No regrets.

If you don't do it this time, then nothing will change. There will be no accomplishment.

Right now you're already ahead of other people who want to write a book because you've already made a start by reading this eBook. So while others don't know how to do it, you do. So many would-be authors want to start writing a book but have no clue how to begin and remain stuck in blank page syndrome.

Or they begin, but soon feel that it's too hard because they really don't know what they're doing.

You, on the other hand, have the solution right in this eBook. And by the time you've worked your way through to the end of it, you'll have your manuscript written.

Just remember though, that passively reading this eBook won't help you. You need to go through it again and actually do the work.

Procrastination is one of the biggest problems that writers face. They put off doing their writing and busy themselves with things that don't matter. This is because starting anything seems hard, especially a big project like writing a book. But I always find that once I do start something (no matter what it is) as soon as I begin, momentum kicks in and it's easy to keep going.

In his book, The War of Art, Author Stephen Pressfield called it Resistance (always spelled with a capital R) and said that if you don't overcome it, Resistance will kill you. It won't upset you or maim you. It will kill you.

But this eBook is all you need to overcome Resistance to getting your book written because it makes the whole process simple and straight forward to follow.

Sci-fi author, Isaac Asimov, who wrote hundreds of novels, when asked how he managed to write so many books said "I guess I'm prolific because I have a simple and straightforward style." And while that is true, the opposite could also be true. Perhaps he needed a simple and straightforward style in order to be prolific.

And it's what you're going to learn. Using the One Month Author simple and straightforward technique of writing a book, will help you to master the whole process from start to finish, which will help you to master proficiency, which will effortlessly give you the speed you need to write a book in a month.

But none of it will work if you give in to Resistance. Don't let it kill you.

Pick a writing schedule and stick to it. Keep your writing hours strictly for writing, and don't give in and do other things instead. Stick to your writing hours like you do to your working hours at your job.

The problem with sticking to a writing schedule is just like when you try and do anything worthwhile. The universe will put obstacles in your way. Try not to let it put you off.

Deal with the urgent things and let the rest go.

I always think that when blockages and obstacles are thrown at me when I'm busy doing something, it means that what I'm doing is worthwhile. It's like a test to see how badly I want to do something.

I also used to find that whenever I was busy writing, other people thought I was selfish. Some even called me boring because I'd rather stay home and write, than go out drinking with them, or go to their place for coffee.

Now that I write for a living, the pressure from others has lessened, although there are still those who never quite understand what I do. But years ago it felt like the universe was throwing other people's bad attitudes at me when I was working hard at trying to get my writing career started.

To become an author takes ambition, commitment, drive and motivation.

Don't let anything or anyone or time constraints stand in your way, even if the only time and place you have to write is in bed at night.

Dealing with obstacles may seem hard, but writing your book won't be. Just follow the process in this eBook and your manuscript will almost write itself. You'll have your finished manuscript in just a few days from now.

Once you start writing, don't stop. Never skip a day. Commit to your daily writing schedule and stick to it. Never say you can't be bothered, or you're too tired. Sit down and write anyway. If you skip just one day, it's too easy to skip the next, and the next.

Never give in to procrastination. Never give in to Resistance. Write every day whether you feel like it or not. Don't wait for your muse to turn up before you write. Your muse won't turn up for work until you do.

Just start. Once you begin using the monthly writing method, it will be so easy, it's fun.

And in the next Chapter we'll begin by choosing a topic to write about.

Even if you have a topic in mind, or you already know what you want to write about, don't skip the next chapter. It's full of inspiring ideas.

Chapter 4.

Choosing a Topic

Choosing a topic to write about isn't difficult. Once you start looking you'll find plenty of ideas.

But whether or not you already know what you want to write about, or you need to find an idea first, there's one crucial thing you need to know.

The topic you choose to write about must be something that readers want to know about.

And while that may sound stupidly simple, don't confuse what they want with what they NEED. In other words it must be something they desire to learn more about. Just because they need to know something doesn't mean they want to read a whole book about it. Don't write a book that no one wants to read.

To make sure you choose a good topic, ask what readers want to know, not what you want to write.

A good way to do this is to ask yourself how you'd advertise your book to potential readers. What would you write in the back cover blurb that would make them want to open your book? How will reading your book help them? What will they gain? How will it entertain them?

Keeping these questions in mind will help you to choose a great topic. And having a great topic will help you write a best seller.

So where do you start with your topic selection?

Start with your own life experiences. No one wants to know your whole life story, but there might be something that happened to you that might help others too. It doesn't have to be anything too out of the ordinary. It can be something as simple as your job, parenting, divorce, gardening, cooking, travel, investing, a disability, running a business, a hobby.

You also need a great title, one that creates curiosity. For instance, if you wanted to write about how you transformed your garden, your title might be, "How I Turned My Garden Into an Eco Sanctuary," Or if you're a parent it might be "How To Get Your Baby to Sleep Through The Night." Now that's a book most new parents would want to read.

You can also use acronyms to drive curiosity like "Start You Day Right With The 6 Morning S.A.V.E.R.S."

Your book title needs to tell the reader what the book is about as well as being intriguing and positive. For instance, I have a book called "How To Quit Smoking Without Giving Up Cigarettes." It's intriguing and positive because people don't want to give up cigarettes, even though they do want to quit smoking, so this title gets them wondering how they can do both.

Questions can also make great titles because it makes readers want to know the answer. For instance there's a self-help book called "Who Moved My Cheese?"

Or there's always the well known two words to start a title "How To...." As in "How To Win Friends And Influence People." Everyone wants to know how to do something.

For fiction books, you probably already know the genre you want to write. Usually the types of novels you like to read are the ones you want to write. One way to get a really good insight, is to look at a few books by your favourite authors and see how they write. Read their books like a writer, not a reader.

Your topic of choice must be something that you're interested in or at least something you can get temporarily enthusiastic about. Don't choose to write about a subject/genre that bores you. Your boredom will show in your writing.

Your topic needs to be popular, but not too popular that there's too many competing books on the subject.

To differentiate your book from other similar books, tighten your subject matter. So to go back to the subject of parenting and babies in particular, your book can be a specific part of having a baby. How to get a baby to sleep through the night.

To choose your topic wisely, go with your instinct. If you love reading horror novels, write one yourself. If you love cooking, write a cook book.

To get readers really interested and make more sales, write a series of books. Readers love to buy books by the same author.

Some authors write several series of books on different topics and use a different pseudonym for each topic to create a following for each series.

So it's worth considering how you can expand one topic into a whole series of books.

Chapter 5.

How To Write Quickly

Now comes the fun part because you're about to learn how to write quickly. I love writing fast because it keeps me in the writing 'flow' and so the ideas keep coming fast and I can capture them straight into my writing. And in just one month I'm the author of a new book.

It's also possible to expand the knowledge you've gained from writing your book, into a blog or website. Many authors set up a site as a place to promote and sell their books. They also talk about the book they're currently writing to make readers eager to buy it once it's published. This is called pre-selling.

If your book is non-fiction you can set up a blog or website on that topic and earn extra money from it. You can also join online groups and casually mention your book, as long as it doesn't come across as a sales pitch. You could say something like "I actually did a lot of research an that subject when I was writing my book, and I found out that..." See how that works? You mentioned the book while talking about something else that relates to your books topic.

But before you can do any of this, you need to write your book, and you want to do it quickly. In a month. That's why you're reading this eBook.

To write quickly means to write simply and not try and use lots of extraneous words. The way to do it is simple. Write As You Speak (WAYS).

Writing quickly stops you from editing as you write and doesn't give you time to second-guess what you're trying to say. Your writing will read as though you actually said it which means it will be easier to understand.

Good writing is simply writing the way you talk and that always means writing quickly. And just like anything we do in life, if we do it often we're able to do it quickly with very little thinking required.

We also speed up writing by using an outline. Some say that working this way stifles creativity, but I find it has the opposite effect.

We have two different halves of our brain. The left side, which is for logical thinking and the right side which is our creative brain.

An outline is written using the left logical part of our brain, which frees up the creative side to do the writing, with no left brain, criticisms or over-analysing. Having less need for logic means more freedom of intuition and makes it so easy to use **WAYS**.

And to speed up writing even more, as you're going to see, we're going to create not just an outline, but we're going to turn it into a blueprint, a list of questions so that all you have to do is answer them and your book will be written.

But how fast can you actually write?

To show you, I'm going to give you a five-minute writing challenge. And you **MUST** do it.

Don't skip this part because you need to know how powerful it is and you'll see how it will revolutionise the way you write.

So right now if you don't already have a pen and paper, go get them, or if you're on your computer, open a blank document, It doesn't matter which way you want to do it, just be sure to do it. Don't skip this 5 minute writing challenge because it's crucial to your success.

So here's what I want you to do.

It only takes 3 words to create a story, and that is what you're going to do.

Take this seriously and follow the rules. Don't skip this and don't cheat.

You need pen and paper or an open document on a computer, and a 5 minute timer.

You need to speed write for 5 minutes as fast as you can. Don't stop. But when the 5 minutes is up you MUST stop immediately. Don't think, don't edit, don't read. Just keep writing. Now in a minute you're going to choose your 3 words. Your writing must begin with one of the 3 words, and the other 2 words must be in your first paragraph. Have you got that? Good.

Here are 3 groups of words: -

1. Woman, library, dancer, ship, darkness, rumour, hinges, chair, clock.
2. Tick, grass, blue, candle, skull, daylight, river, turkey, puppet.
3. Reindeer, rumpus, dinner, havok, dream, people, drink, plate, forest.

Now you need to think of 3 dates. The first is today's date, the second is your birth date, and the third is a meaningful date to you, either a child's birth date, your wedding date, or another date that means something to you.

For each of these dates you need to add up the day, month and year, and keep adding until you have a single number. So for instance, if today's date is 27th July 2021, It would be 27 + 07 + 2021 = 2055 = 2 + 0+ 5 + 5 = 12 = 1 + 2 = 3.

So your first number would be 3. Then do the same for the other 2 dates.

For your first number choose the corresponding word in the first list. So if you're number 3, the word would be 'dancer' because it's the third word in the first list. Choose your second number from the second list, and your third from the third list. Now start your timer for 5 minutes and start writing. Remember, the first word you write must be one of your 3 words, and the other 2 must both be in your first paragraph.

Start your timer now and start writing.

STOP. Now your 5 minutes is up and you should have written 2/3 of a page. Isn't it amazing how much you can write in only 5 minutes.

Plus your mind is free and more creative when you're speed writing.

If you can write quickly like you just did it means you could write a 400-page book in 25 hours. Now that's fast. And you only needed 3 words to get started.

Now read what you've written, it should be pretty good. Not bad for 5 minutes with only 3 random words and no thinking time. In fact it could even be the best you've ever written.

Beginning with one of your chosen words (a noun) is starting with a power word that gets your story straight to the point instantly.

Can you see how this 5 minute writing exercise with clear directions and a deadline eliminated writers block? So simple yet so powerful.

And now you know how to write fast which means you can produce work in a fraction of the time it used to take. Writing without thinking is so easy to do with an outline, even if it's only 3 words.

Too much thinking causes writer's block and also creates poor writing. On the other hand, as you just seen, speedwriting makes your work easy to understand.

But what if you didn't produce 2/3 page of easy to understand writing? Then do it again with 3 different words. You were thinking, not writing.

Just like using the 3 words, outlining speeds up your writing and makes your writing better. It also means you can easily write a book in a month. You can even write it faster depending on the time you have available to write and the length of your book.

Writing 400 pages in 25 hours (and that would be a **REALLY** long book), writing for just one hour a day, means you'd have your manuscript finished in 25 days. And not many books are that long. In fact, most are much shorter.

And repeating the book-writing process is easy once you've done it, especially now you know how fast you can write in 5 minutes even without practice.

Chapter 6.

The Plot Thickens

Now that you know how to write fast, we're now going to talk about what you'll be writing and we're going to begin by looking at plots.

Now I know what you're thinking. Only fiction books have plots, that is true, but this method of plotting that we're going to look at works for non-fiction too.

Having an intriguing plot is part of the outlining process, and it's this creativity that makes writing fun.

A plot for your book doesn't have to be a single idea. It can be an ongoing thread that runs through a whole series of books. Each story must stand alone yet at the same time the plot follows on.

A good example of this is the well known Harry Potter books. Each book can be read entirely on it's own and is a complete story. But as the series progresses many hidden sub-plots emerge that hadn't been apparent before.

There can also be continuing plots in non-fiction books such as the 3-book series:

>
> Buddhism For Busy People
>
> Hurry Up And Meditate
>
> Enlightenment To Go

With these three books you can do one of these things quickly and squeeze it into your life, or you can transform your life with all three.

Again, each book stands completely on it's own or all 3 can be strung together.

Fiction books always need a strong and intriguing plot. Many publishers reject books because of a bad plot, not because of bad writing.

Events need to follow through from one to the next to the next to create a whole story from beginning, to a crisis or two, and then to a satisfactory ending. The plot needs to build curiosity. Readers need to care what happens and for that they need to identify with the characters. You can read about how to create characters in chapter 10.

A novel needs to contain the 4 C's

Characters

Conflict

Crisis

Change

It begins with mapping out the characters bios. You can't make them real unless you understand who they are, what drives them, and how they came to be in the situation they're in.

Next is conflict. Something must happen that sends them on an unexpected journey in their life. The conflict often comes from a character's flaw, a weakness or fear.

Crisis. There's usually more than one crisis in a story and typically there are three. They all lead to an ultimate crisis and can happen to more than one character.

Lastly there is change, either physical, emotional, or both. But it needs to satisfy and make the reader feel it was worth reading the whole story to get to this point. There is usually a romantic ending too even if there wasn't one before.

When you're trying to find a plot for your novel, remember that there are no new plot's. Every story is the same plot presented differently.

Don' believe me? Look at the plot of the old TV series My Favourite Martian, a comedy about an alien who lived on earth and pretended he was human. Only one person knew who he really was.

A few years later there was Mork and Mindy. Mork was an alien living on earth, pretending to be human and only one person, Mindy, knew who he really was.

Then there was Alf, and then 3rd Rock From the Sun which was only different because it was a group of aliens pretending to be a family.

And what about the 2 movies, War of the Worlds and Independence Day? Both are about aliens who tried to take over the earth and are killed by a virus. In War of the Worlds, it was a human virus, in Independence Day it was a computer virus.

Whatever plot you want for your book, it's been done before, just not in the same way you're going to do it.

If you don't have a plot, no problem. You can buy one.

Go to a secondhand bookstore and buy a novel that's at least 3 to 9 years old so that the plot isn't current. It does not matter too much about the genre of the book. If you buy an old best seller you'll know that you have a best selling plot. But any book will do as long as the plot looks intriguing.

Read the book and write out the plot. Use it for a book of your own. Don't plagiarise. Change things about the plot including the characters, the time period, the location and even the genre. If you've chosen a romance book, turn the plot into a Who Dunnit, or a sci-fi into a modern day mystery.

The plot you develop must be unrecognizable from the original book.

This is a really fun exercise and gets the creative juices overflowing.

If your going to write a non-fiction book, find books on the same topic you're interested in and see what subjects the chapters cover for ideas of your own.

Add chapters that explain obstacles and challenges the reader will face and how to overcome them.

Non-fiction books are written as a solution to a problem. Start your book with the problem and, just like in the fiction books, end with change.

For a book to be successful, you have to know what the reader wants and the benefit they're looking for.

You can even take an already successful book title and give it a different focus, such as, "Think and Grow Rich For Students." Not a great example but you get the idea.

A good plot is crucial for both fiction and non-fiction. A fiction book leads the reader from the beginning of a story to a satisfactory ending. A non-fiction book takes a reader from a problem to a solution.

In your book, always answer the question why? In fiction, why did they do that? In non-fiction, why should they do that? There needs to be a happily-ever-after (HEA) ending for both types of books. In fiction it's a HEA for the characters, and in non-fiction a HEA for the reader.

Read book reviews of the type of book you want to write because they tell you what the readers liked, what they didn't like, and what they thought was missing.

Once you've found your plot it's easy to work it into a complete story. All you have to do is improve on what's already been written.

Plus, things always change so stories can be updated and information always changes too.

In some older books, writers were told to research at the library. Now they're told to do it online.

Writing was also more about manual labour of carrying around research books and notebooks. Now it's all about computers.

But the plots always stay the same so you can look for your best seller.

Chapter 7.

Research Fast

When your in the planning stages of writing a book, it's too easy to get caught up in over-researching, and that can be a relentless loop to get stuck in.

You don't need to know everything about a subject. Doctors don't know every single thing there is to know about the subject of medicine, Lawyers don't know every single thing about law. Likewise, you don't need to know every single thing about a subject you want to write about. You need to know it well, but you don't need to know everything.

Over-researching is a waste of time and a huge distraction. It's also a form of procrastination. So only do the research you need and then get on with writing your book.

Likewise, when you're writing, don't overload your readers with information they don't need to know. You don't need to include too many specifics. You're writing from your own perspective, not unloading a whole warehouse of information on your reader.

If you know your subject well, you can write first, and do the research later. Just leave blank spaces if there's something you don't know and a list of research questions. You should only have a short list of questions.

Finding answers to a list of specific questions is much faster than trying to do general research when you don't know exactly what you're looking for.

One of the fastest places I've ever found to do research is in the children's section of the library.

You can go there and research or read the books online, if they're available digitally.

Children's reference books explain things so simply and succinctly and are far more easy to understand than adult books. Adult reference books are usually aimed at students writing essays and thesis, so they are crammed with detailed information, most of which is unnecessary for the average person.

Children's books on the other hand, get straight to the point and explain things so that, well, even a child can understand.

So before you start researching, know the questions before you try and find the answers. Once you've found the answer, stop researching. You must know when to stop. You already have all the information you need for the rest of your book. Writing first gives specific questions for speedy research.

And when you do research, don't use old books and outdated information, unless of course you're researching the history of how something used to be done.

State the sources of your information for more authority.

When you find the answer to a question, ask why and answer it. Something may be true or necessary, but why? You can give your own perspective on the reasoning which gives your book unique information that no other book has. Also, how does the information benefit the reader?

If you're writing fiction, ask why are your characters doing what they're doing?

Readers have questions when they're reading and asking yourself why, answer those questions for them.

Putting this altogether creates a unique book with information that no other book has. And using WAYS keeps it simple to understand, interesting, and entertaining.

Using WAYS, answering questions, and putting your own unique perspective in a book, can all be done by speed writing. And fast research means you can write a book in a month – or less.

And when you've done it once, you'll have perfected your own way of writing making it easier and faster next time.

And now we'll do another writing exercise (last one, I promise) so that you can see how easy it is to write on any subject, even one that you don't know too much about. This exercise is also about coming up with questions to answer.

I'm going to give you a list of possible subjects that at first may seem not at all interesting, but once you start thinking you'll discover how easy it is to find interesting questions to ask about it.

So, here is the list of possible subjects: -

    chairs

    carpets

    parrots

    apples

    planes

    paper

    rats

    elevators

    sand

Choose one word from the list. If you can't decide, make your choice the same way you did for the previous exercise. Add up the numbers from your date of birth, and choose the corresponding word from the list.

Write down your chosen word and then think of 10 possible questions to ask about it. Don't research this, Just think, and come up with the questions yourself.

For instance, for chairs you could ask "what are they made of?" For sand you could ask "what is it used for in the construction industry?

Write down 10 questions about your word.

Times Up. Now that your finished, look at your questions. They will be better than you thought because even with a subject you don't know much about, it's still possible to come up with 10 questions which could make 10 interesting chapters in a book.

And it's this same technique that is used in outlining a book manuscript, which is what we are going to do next.

So get ready because this is where the work begins.

Chapter 8.

Create a Book Outline

This is the start of the fun stuff. Some people call it hard work and while that may be the case for a few people, I think it's fun. Writing an outline gets the creative part of the brain working which is always preferable to working with the logic left brain.

Using an outline makes sure that all necessary topics are covered, and that they're in the correct order. This also makes writing a book much faster, and outlining is just as creative as writing, and I find that it makes the writing more fun.

The outline is the most important part of writing and it allows you to get your topics in order and ready to be written out in greater detail.

A poor outline produces a poor book. Some people think that outlining is a waste of time and that it's easier and faster to just make a few notes and then get on with the writing. But I disagree.

Using an outline helps in actually getting the book done, streamlines the writing process and helps to present the information in the best way possible.

And it doesn't matter whether you're writing fiction or non-fiction because the process is the same.

So let's get down to work.

The average amount of pages per chapter in a book is 10. That isn't set in stone and chapters can have more or less pages, but for the purpose of writing a book, we'll stick with 10 pages.

So how many chapters does a book have?

Different Genres have different amounts of chapters. For instance literary novels are usually huge tomes (400+ pages) and around 40 chapters, while a children's novel is only around 15 chapters (150 pages).

Here is a list of genres and expected lengths.

Genre	Pages	Chapters
Literary Novel	400	40
Romance	350	35
Horror	350	35
Fantasy	350	35
Sci-Fi	300	30
Crime	280	28
Adventure	280	28
Pulp Romance	240	24
Western	200	20
How To	200	20
Teen Novel	200	20
Age 9-12 Novel	150	15
Hollywood Script	100	10

All these chapter numbers are average, except Westerns which must be exactly 20 chapters.

Now take a piece of paper and a pen or open a blank document on your computer. I always find it easier to outline by hand so that I can spread the pages out and see them all and do all my scribbling, additions and changes myself. But each to their own way.

On the left-hand side of the page write down Chapter 1, Chapter 2, etc. 18 chapters in all.

Now just like you did in the previous exercise when you had to think of 10 different things to discuss about one subject, write down 18 different things to discuss about the topic of your book. Remember you already chose your topic back in chapter 4. So now you need a key topic for each chapter. Your book will also have an introduction, or preface, and a conclusion, so you'll have 20 chapters altogether.

So for instance, if your book is about Hotel Management, some of your chapters might be Concierge Service, Housekeeping, Room Service.

For fiction each chapter must move the plot forward and intrigue the reader about what will happen next, It also needs setting, characterization, and must have plot development to take the reader deeper into the story. So for instance your first chapter (at this stage) could be, David starts a new job.

Once you have your list of chapters and a brief description of what it's about, you then expand each chapter into 18 different points/topics.

For instance, the chapter on Housekeeping could include, Equipment, Security, Hiring Staff, Staff Training, Laundry.

I feel that I should add here that I know nothing at all about hotel management, so I'm only guessing at what a book about it would contain.

For fiction, the first chapter of, David begins a new job, could expand to David's work is hard. Has an argument with his new boss. Discovers staff thefts.

If you find that you have more than 18 topics, you need an extra chapter.

If you can't think of 18, use the 6 W's which are. Who? What? When? Where? Why? How? Ask these questions of what you've already written. And yes, I know that they don't all begin with a W, but it makes it easier to remember them if I pretend they do.

When you've finished listing all 18 topics for 18 chapters, subtract 3 from each chapter. Remove the ones that are least useful or least interesting. Next, arrange the remaining 15 into the most logical order.

This whole process is easy to talk about but does take a bit of time to do. In the end you'll have quite a few dozen pages of outline.

What you have when you've finished is the best order for all your chapters and the information or story they contain.

Whatever you do, don't skip any of these steps. You'll see why later and you'll understand why it's so important.

And believe it or not, the hardest part of writing a book is now over.

You now have all your chapters, topics, story, plot, and characters.

And next it's time to turn your outline into a blueprint.

Chapter 9.

From Outline To Blueprint To Manuscript.

Now that you've completed your manuscript, it's time to expand it into a blueprint.

Why?

Because a blueprint will guide your writing every step, leaving you free to write quickly, confidently, and tap into your full right-brain creativity.

I know right now that you've already spent a lot of time creating your outline. But don't worry because most of the work is done so there isn't much more to do.

To turn your outline into a blueprint, we need to go back to what we practiced earlier when you had to come up with 10 questions to ask about your topic.

So now take your 15 topics for each chapter and turn each one into a question.

Write your 15 topic questions on the left side of the page and leave 3 lines below each one. Do this for every chapter of your book.

So for example, in the Hotel Management book, the topic of housekeeping equipment would become What types of equipment are needed?

In the fiction example, David starts a new job, could become Why did David start a new job? Or What happened when David arrived on his first day of work?

If you're writing fiction, your story also needs a viewpoint. It can stay the same throughout the story or it can change.

There's first person viewpoint which is told through the eyes of the main character, or third person which is all about the main character and his feelings, but is not told directly through them, or omnipresent viewpoint which is as though the whole story is told from an all-seeing narrator. This type of narrator viewpoint isn't popular, but it can work depending on the story.

The beginning of your book must grab the reader's attention and create curiosity.

Also keep your characters always moving forward. They need to be doing something, even when they're talking. This is a trick done in TV shows and movies all the time.

The characters are always walking, driving and even travelling on an aeroplane when they're talking. If they're at home they're doing the dishes, or trending the garden, or any number of other things when they're talking to someone else. Even if a police detective comes to interview them, they still never stop doing what they're doing.

And it's the same in books. As long as your characters are doing something it feels like the story is progressing too. Fiction always needs plenty of emotion too. Readers like to feel a story as well as read it. If there's no emotion the reader won't feel anything and will close the book.

Even in non-fiction the reader needs to feel emotion. It always needs to be positive emotion so that they feel good about reading and learning something and moving towards their happily ever after too.

When you've changed all your topics into questions, go through them from the beginning and on the 3 blank lines write 3 answers.

Take your time doing this, don't rush it. Your answers don't have to be long. Just one word will do. It's only going to be you who needs to understand what you write, so if all you feel you need is 3 single words as answers to a question then that's sufficient.

For example, in the Hotel Management book, one of the answers to What type of equipment is needed, could be 'Dusting.' To anyone else that might not mean much, but to you it could mean anything to do with cleaning a hotel room such as duster, polish, long-handle duster, microfibre cloths, disinfectant, air freshener, rubber gloves.

Remember, these answers are important because they are the skeleton of your book.

So take your time.

When you've finished, it's time for the really, REALLY fun part, and that is, writing your book. And you're going to write it in the fastest way possible.

Are you ready?

Then here we go.

All you have to do is work your way through each question and write out the 3 answers. Use the timer like you did in the previous 5 minute challenge. You should write 2/3 page in 5 minutes just as you did before.

This means that if you write all 15 topics at 2/3 page each you'll be writing 10 pages per chapter. This also means that you'll write a chapter in 75 minutes.

So if you're writing 20 chapters, it will take 1,500 minutes (75 minutes x 20 chapters) and that's 25 hours.

So even if you took the same amount of time to work your way through idea to planning to outlining to blueprint, that would be 50 hours in total. Many people work this much in one week (5 days), but you've got 30 days to do it.

Chapter 10.

Creating Characters.

This chapter is all about creating believable characters in your fiction book.

A novel needs characters and conflict to drive the story. To have a successful book, your readers must identify with your characters whether they're good or bad. They need to care about the characters and care about what happens to them, even if they're waiting for a villain to get what they deserve, they need to care enough to hope he gets it.

A story needs more than one character. There needs to be the main character/s and minor characters, although in some books, it's one main character battling a non-human enemy. In Stephen King's novel, The Girl Who Loved Tom Gordon, it was about a girl who is lost in the woods and so the villain was the environment. She was lost, hungry and scared. He also wrote a story about a man who was shipwrecked on a tiny island that was nothing but rocks. To survive, he had to cut of parts of his body and eat them. So that story also had one character who was battling starvation, pain and his environment. Luckily he was a surgeon with a scalpel and plenty of alcohol.

But no matter how few or how many characters are in the story, each one of them must speak and act consistently, so you need to know them well.

To do this you need to outline a bio for each one. For the main character you need to know as much as you can about them. For minor characters you don't need to know as much. Only what is necessary for the story.

A detailed bio must contain as much information as you can, even if some of it is never mentioned in the story you still need it to know the character well. So include name, age, married? kids? Job, speech, likes, dislikes, fears, regrets, eating, drinks, holidays.

Find 3 words that sun up your character well and that gives a good three-dimensional overview of them. It must be 3 words. Less than that and all you have is a cartoon character – Sleepy, Grumpy, Happy.

Each character needs a flaw. No one is perfect. Often the flaw is something they eventually need to overcome in the final crisis of the story.

A story also needs a love component. It must end with a love story. It can be a lover, love for a child or even an aged relative. They need to end with a strong emotional bond with someone.

Point of View (POV) is also important in a story as to whose point the story is told from. As we previously discussed it can be an omnipresent view, "The sun rose over the sleepy town, just as Lila ran down the street." Or first person "I ran down the street.: Or third person "Lila ran down the street." It's usual for the story to be told from the main characters POV, but stories can be told by multiple viewpoints too, so that you see a scene from the hero's POV, and then see it again from the protagonists POV to show how they have different reasons for what they're doing. And how differently they view their interactions with each other.

Another important thing to consider about your characters, is their personality traits. This is different from their bio and has a direct effect on their motivations.

No one is perfect and no one is all bad or good. That's a fact of life.

There are three personality traits, and we all have three, but in differing degrees. The three different types are – good, bad, neutral.

A neutral trait is somewhat controversial because it can be negative or positive depending on the circumstance. For instance, 'impatience' can be viewed as a negative personality trait, yet it may be what drives someone to success. So depending on what your character's doing at the time, a neutral personality trait can equally help them or harm them.

With the good and bad traits, each personality contains two.

Here is how that works in personalities:

    Very Good – 2 positive + 1 neutral

    Good – 2 positive + 1 negative

    Normal – 1 positive + 1 negative + 1 neutral

    Bad – 2 negative + 1 positive

    Very bad – 2 negative + 1 neutral

Giving your characters at least one negative (or neutral) trait gives them a weakness or a flaw, and real people have these. Even if a bad character has one positive trait or one neutral trait, it can be a flaw that is their total undoing.

Personality traits give characters internal conflicts and makes them interesting.

A story doesn't have to be action-packed to be interesting. The psychology of watching a person's internal struggles because of their personality traits can be just as interesting, if not more.

Characters drive a story, and we love to read about their emotional struggles. And their character flaws don't have to be huge to create a story. They can be everyday internal struggles that many people face.

For instance, someone wants to move to the country and live of the land to avoid working a 9-5 job in the city. Or an industrious person can also be lazy because they want to write a book, but they want to do it quickly and easily.

What makes a lot of characters popular and memorable is not only a solid bio and interesting character traits, they also have an ongoing habit, or pet phrase. "Do you feel lucky punk?" "Missed it by that much."

Chapters in a novel are made up of several scenes, each one involving a circumstance that a character finds themselves in. A scene can be a heated conversation, a chase, breaking into a house, an intimate bedroom scene, or even a meal shared by several characters. Think of a scene in a book as being the same as in a movie. If it means a change of characters or a change of setting, it's a scene.

Each scene needs what is known as PACE. People, Action, Conversation, Emotion.

Conversation can be internal or external. Have you ever noticed in movies and on TV, there is always action? Something physical is always happening. Even when characters are having a conversation, they're doing something else at the same time. Driving, eating, walking.

Good examples are, on the TV show, The Big Bang Theory, throughout the whole 10 years of the show, the elevator in their building was out of order, so they always had to take the stairs, and talked as they walked. On Criminal Minds they always took their private jet to whatever city they went to and discussed the case as they flew.

On TV and Movie detective shows, when the police question people in their homes, they never stop doing whatever they're doing and will speak to the detectives while cleaning, or packing, or gardening, or cooking. All these things are designed to give the illusion of the story moving forward. Conversation without action feels static.

This happens in books too. Not only is there movement during dialogue, but there's also visible emotion like tears welling in eyes, raised eyebrows, hurt looks or even sweating.

In each scene always know how it makes the point of view character feel, even if you don't describe it, so that the reader can identify with them.

Setting for the whole book is also important. The reader needs to know what country the story is taking place in as well as what town or what city. It's no good writing a story about a haunted house if no one knows where it is. Where the story is talking place should become known in the first chapter. You don't necessarily have to describe it in detail. And you don't have to 'set the scene' first. Of course, you can do this if it helps. Otherwise, the setting can become known accidently or coincidentally through the narrative.

In old books they used to ramble on about the setting right at the beginning. Sometimes it would go on for a page or two. That was probably because people didn't travel as much back then, and often not at all. So they had to have enough information upfront to know exactly what it looked like and to get a real 'feel' for the place.

I think it's also important that your book's setting needs to be known to you, otherwise you won't understand how people live there. Unless of course, you're writing a sci-fi novel and your setting is fictitious.

Horror novelist, Stephen King, wrote his settings for nearly all his books as taking place in Maine in the US, because this is where he lives and so he knows it well, even right down to local accents, the weather, and the quirks of the local people.

Chapter 11.

Editing To Perfection

Your book is written. Now it's time to edit it to make it the best it can be. If you've followed the outlining, blueprinting and writing process, then there shouldn't be much that needs changing. No book is ever perfect, but you can get it close.

Every author has the same problem when it comes to editing, and that is, it never seems to be perfect.

But that's because it never will be. You can go on editing it every day for the rest of your life, and you'll always find something that you think is wrong. That's why you should only edit it once and call, it done.

Speedwriting always produces better writing so that makes the editing faster too. You have limited time to edit so don't get too hung up on trying to be a perfectionist.

What you're looking for, is that your book reads clearly. As long as you can read through it and understand it, then it's good.

Just remember that you're only trying to make sure it's good enough. Too much editing brings diminishing returns.

Don't even try and edit your work until you've finished it. If you want to see it with "fresh eyes," leave it for a day after you've finished it and don't even think about it.

Because you used the speedwriting technique to write your book, editing shouldn't take more than an afternoon. With so few errors, there'll be little to do. If you've written a large novel, you'll need a whole day to edit it.

Use find-and-replace to look for words ending in ly. These are usually adverbs. Replace them with a stronger word, or remove them completely.

So if you've written, "he ran quickly," remove the adverb. It's unnecessary. Or change the verb and say he sprinted or he bolted.

Replace "have to" to "must." It's a stronger word. Replace other weak words, including almost, nearly, usually, virtually, about. Be more accurate.

Use a page break at the end of each chapter and begin each chapter as a new page.

As you go through it, if any paragraph needs work, mark it and go back and correct it once you've finished editing.

Cliché's are lazy writing. Don't use them. E.g. "he was the font of all knowledge."

Remember, edit once. Don't go over it again.

Use the Hemmingway app to find any instances of passive voice in case you've missed some.

I can't tell you enough how important it is to not get hung up on editing and trying to be perfect. Don't do it. Good enough is good enough.

Your readers are looking for a great story regardless of whether your book is fiction or non-fiction. If it's fiction they're looking for entertainment. In non-fiction they want infotainment.

Make sure your book reads smoothly and is easy to understand. If you stumble over a sentence, so will your reader, so fix it.

Write fast and edit faster.

Chapter 12.

Writing Your Own Life Story

We're all familiar with celebrities writing their own life story, otherwise known as an autobiography.

These books sell well because so many people are interested in the life of their favourite celebrity.

There are also non-celebrities who also want to write a book about their life because they feel that it holds a story worth telling.

Unlike autobiographies of the rich and famous, these life stories don't prominently feature the author's name on the cover because no one knows who they are, so they don't care. Instead, the title of it will feature a benefit of reading it like, "How I Quit Sugar" or "How I Lost 80 Pounds in 6 Months."

If you've ever wanted to write a book about your own life story, you must be an interesting person with an interesting story to tell about your life, or have had a one-off life changing experience.

Everyone wants to read the life story of a famous person, because their lives are so different from ours. But no one wants to read about the life of an ordinary person unless it contains an important, teachable moment. It also needs a positive ending that leaves the reader uplifted and hopeful.

Before you even begin to write your life story, make sure it will contain all those things - an interesting person, an interesting life with at least one life-changing experience that is a teachable moment., and an uplifting, hopeful ending for the reader.

I remember years ago, a woman sent me a few chapters of her manuscript and a synopsis and asked if I would be interested in publishing her book. The title was something like. "My Husband Was The Best Ever." The book was the story of how she met and married her husband years ago. Then recently he went on holiday with his mates, got into a drunken fight and was murdered. She felt that the whole world needed to know what a great husband he had been and what a shame it was that he was killed.

I was flabbergasted. Why would anyone want to read a whole book about that? How was he such a great husband if they had separate holidays? And I was sure that most women think their husband is the best. They wouldn't want to read a book telling them it wasn't true because this guy was the best. I couldn't see any value in reading this woman's story of how she lost her husband, as sad as it was.

So why am I telling you about this? To show you that even though a story is tragic, and the death of a spouse is such a huge event in life, it doesn't mean it's an interesting story, and it's not teachable either. Even if this story was written by someone who nearly died this way, it may be newsworthy to a journalist, but it's not book-worthy to a reader.

But if you have a story that others are intrigued by because they want to do the same, or are entertained by, because it's a really funny story, then you've got a winner.

To keep the pace of your story moving swiftly, and to make it read like a story (as opposed to a list of events), write in the present tense. Also write in the first person.

If there are any dead characters in your story, write as if they're still alive to keep your story uplifting. No one wants to read a story that sounds like an obituary. It's ok to have a few sad moments, but overall your story must be uplifting.

As you tell your story make the reader feel as though they're right there with you in the present, along for the ride, living it all with you.

Don't be negative about anything, and don't complain. That comes across as whining. Say what happened (or what is happening, you're writing in the present tense) but don't give your own negative opinion about it, no matter how bad it was/is.

Write as the person you were at the time each thing happened, not who you are now. Arrange your story creatively. It doesn't have to be chronological.

Give it a beginning, and end, and 3 major middle parts. If you can't come up with 3, then maybe your story isn't interesting enough for a book.

Even if you're writing about a simple subject like weight-loss, your 3 major pats might be How you began, including how you decided what to do, how physically difficult it was and when it got easier, and how your attitude went from miserable to light and happy. Each one of these could have a crisis like how you nearly gave up, or how it was consuming your every waking moment, and how you had to buy new clothes all the time as your weight changed.

When you have your 3 major middle parts, number them from least interesting to most interesting.

Write the most interesting first, the least interesting second, and the second most interesting last so that your story starts off great and ends good.

You'll find that it takes a lot of creative thought to organise a true story this way. No life story, no matter how you tell it, will be strictly chronological. Sometimes you need to look back and other times you'll have to skip forward. At times you'll also need to admit your weakness or accept your mistakes in life.

You'll also discover that writing your autobiography can be one of the greatest acts of self-discovery. Anyone who journals knows this. Events and attitudes can be seen more clearly when you write about it.

Your life story should be about events that happened a long time ago. If the events are too recent, they're too fresh on your memory and so you'll try and include too much detail. Details aren't necessary unless they're pertinent to the story. Don't include them just because you remember them.

Keep writing in the present. Don't ever write, "I remember...." That sounds like a long, boring story before you've even begun.

Keep your story positive, it's supposed to be nostalgic, not a lamentation. Bring all your experiences to life in the here and now.

Naturally, your story will include other people because they are/were part of your life and what happened to you. Change their names if necessary, but it's ok to use their real names if they're ok with it too.

Your life story is easy to write because you already know the whole story. You don't need to make up characters and conflicts because they're already there. All you have to do is map it out so it's easy to follow, and make it interesting.

Re-live your life in your story and share it with others so that they can enjoy the ride and learn something new.

Chapter 13.

Marketing & Selling Your Book.

So now your book is written. Believe it or not, that was the easy part.

Don't make the mistake that some authors make and leave your manuscript in a drawer or on your computer. You need to be brave and send it out into the world.

Now that it's written and edited, leave it alone. Don't try and change a thing. Remember that good enough is good enough.

The thing to consider now is how you're going to publish your book. The choice you have is to either try and get it published through a traditional publishing company, or publish it yourself.

If you choose self-publishing, you can do it straight away and get on with writing your next book. If you use traditional publishing, you need to find an agent or submit your work directly to the publishing companies.

To submit to traditional publishers or an agent, you'll need to write a synopsis of your book, which is a summary of what it's about in 1 or 2 pages.

You'll also need a list of chapter outlines, which include the chapter title/number and 1 or 2 sentences. Most agents and publishers also want a few sample chapters. This is often the first 3 chapters.

They also need a covering letter.

Each agent and publishing company is different so they may want all or only some of these things.

A literary agent is someone who submits your book to publishing companies on your behalf and earns money by charging a small percentage of your royalties. They also act as your manager once your book is published.

Many publishing companies only deal with agents and won't accept author submissions.

Both agents and publishing companies only deal with certain genres or subjects, so you need to check their websites to see what they accept, what they want you to send, and whether or not they're currently accepting submissions.

Here's a caveat. Beware of publishing companies that seem to be more about publishing books than selling them. A legitimate publishing company will be all about selling books and their home page on their website will list all their latest books and special offers.

If you find a company whose home page is all about how they want to publish your book, and how they're always open to manuscript submissions, beware.

These are called vanity publishers and what they do is charge authors to publish their books, and the fee is usually one or two thousand dollars or more. In return they promise to sell your book from their website and let other bookstores know about your book. They'll also offer you a great marketing package too, for another high fee, to help you "maximise" your book sales. These companies make money from authors, not from book sales so chances are if you sign up with them the whole publishing process will be simple, expensive, and a total waste of time. But boy do they make their offers attractive and make it sound like a cannot-fail-to-earn-a-million publishing deal.

A legitimate publishing company won't charge you to publish your book and will pay you a small royalty for every sale. These companies tend to work slowly so even if you get a publishing deal with them, it can still be a year or two before your book is published. But they do all the work for you including formatting and cover design.

If you choose to self-publish, you'll have to format the interior of your book yourself. You'll need to add the prelim pages which include the dedication page (if using) and copyright page, plus a Table of Contents if it's a non-fiction book, as well as a disclaimer and any other pages you want at the front or back of your book. For ideas, look inside other books.

Make sure your first chapter begins on a right-hand page if it's a print book.

You'll also need to format your book interior a little bit differently if it's an eBook. It won't matter what page your first chapter starts on, and you need to take out the page numbers.

The type of file you need for your self-published book (Word, PDF, or text document, etc.) depends on where you want to publish it. There are many self-publishing companies, and here are 3 as an example.

Smashwords. This company only publishes eBooks so if this is the only way you want to publish, this company is a good choice. They don't supply book covers so you need to have your own flat front cover image. This is simple to do on your own computer. Design it as a text document (don't forget to give it a background colour) and save it as an image. Smashwords distribute your eBook to online retailers worldwide, including Amazon, and their fee is a percentage from all book sales.

Amazon. This is a company that some authors use solely for publishing their books. Amazons KDP platform allows you to self-publish your book in print format and eBook format (or just one or the other). They provide cover creating software, including a library of images you can choose from, but it's better to use one of your own for individuality. They charge a fee from every book sale.

Ingram Sparks. This company sells books and eBooks worldwide as well as listing books in the catalogues of library supply companies. They also provide cover-creating software for both print and eBooks. Unlike Smashwords and Amazon who are free to self-publish with, Ingram Sparks do charge a small one-off publishing fee, but their distribution has a bigger reach.

All self-publishing companies print books using POD (Print On Demand) technology which means that books aren't printed until they're ordered. Before POD, books had to be printed by the 1,000's and physically shipped to each bookstore. This is why authors couldn't afford to publish their own books.

When you self-publish you set your own price for your books, taking into account the cost of printing. If it's an eBook, the price is pure profit, except for a small handling fee.

If you can get libraries interested in your books or eBooks, this can increase sales dramatically, plus you receive PLR payments (Public Lending Rights) payments whenever your books or eBooks are borrowed or downloaded. Not all countries pay PLR payments to authors, but many do. You'll have to look that up for the country you live in. These amounts and methods of payments often change so I don't want to go into individual information about it here.

Also schools may be interested in your book so it may also be worth contacting the department of education to see if it's a book they want to use or something their libraries might want to stock.

Whether you self-publish your book or opt for traditional publishing, marketing is always left to the author. Many publishing companies want to know how you intend to market your book before they'll sign a contract with you.

However you choose to publish, you need to have a marketing plan. You need to know not just how you're going to sell it, but who you're going to sell it to. Who is your target audience?

Once you know who you want to sell it to you can devise a plan of how you're going to do it.

Come up with a 10 point marketing plan. You need to know 10 different ways you're going to market it.

Pre-marketing can often be a good way to market a book. Let people know that it will soon be available and where they can buy a copy.

Sending out a press release can help and so can talking about it on social media.

If you have a blog or a website (and you really should) it's the best place to talk about an upcoming book. If you have an email list of subscribers, that's even better because you already have your target audience and you can market directly to them. You can tell them how excited you are about your new book and brag about all the things that are going to be in it, or how intriguing the story is if it's a novel.

Marketing must be consistent and ongoing. Once you've published your book, even if it's years later, still keep marketing it at every opportunity.

It's what I call McMarketing. You see, McDonalds, no matter how long they've been around, they never stop marketing because they know how powerful constant marketing can be. They may not sell the best burgers, but their perpetual marketing machine make sure they sell the most, and that their brand is well known.

To market your book you can use paid advertising either online or in magazines. This can be costly and your ads need a really compelling reason why anyone would want to buy your book.

You could also do marketing through writing and submitting freelance articles in magazines or online blogs and websites. This has the advantage of giving you a further reach with your marketing if you mention your book in your byline, but you'll also get paid for writing the article. You could also write an unpaid article for a blog or website if they let you mention your book in your resource box. Just make sure the site is read by your target audience.

There are also online article sites like Medium, where you can upload articles and create a whole new online following. Sites like this have millions of readers, most of whom will never visit your website/blog.

You can also submit articles to online article directories like EzineArticles because they allow you to have an author's resource box which is included at the end of each article. Also others are allowed to publish your articles on their own site/blog, along with your resource box which helps with marketing too.

You can send a copy of your book to review sites and use SEO in all your online marketing to make sure that anyone looking for a book like yours will find it.

People need to know your book is there otherwise they can't buy it.

If you can write a book series that's even better because if readers like your first book they're likely to buy them all.

And I don't think you need to try and get your book onto a best seller list. The aim is to sell as many copies as you can for a long time. Best seller lists only list books that have sold the most copies in a short time. There are many authors who have never been on a best seller list even though they've been writing books for years. Yet they sell more copies of their books than most of those on the best seller lists.

This is because they may not sell them quickly, but they do go on to make thousands more sales and eventually out-sell the best-sellers.

Some of these authors are, JA Konrath, Dean Wesley Smith and Yuwanda Black.

And the one thing these authors have in common, as well as selling lots of books, is that they never stop marketing.

And neither should you.

Chapter 14.

Writing Wrap Up

So now we've come to the end of being a One Month Author.

We've gone from idea to outline to blueprint to manuscript to sales.

Writing and publishing a book is a huge topic and can seem intimidating if you've never done it before.

But I hope by now I've made it more simple and more doable, and most importantly, you now know how you can do it in just a month.

If you work your way through this eBook again and again, each time it will all become easier and faster. You'll know how to outline and write a book, where to publish it, and you won't need to think of a 10-point marketing plan because you'll already have one.

If you can do it in a month, that means you can write and publish 12 books a year. This means that in 5 years you'll be the author of 60 books.

But I know what you're thinking. Is it possible to write that many books that fast and consistently?

Well what about this. Dean Wesley Smith is an author. He's also a monthly author. He writes a book a month and he's done so for years. He even has a huge list of subscribers who pay a monthly fee to receive a copy of every book he writes. They sign up, set up their account so that the money is paid automatically every month, and as an incentive to stay subscribed they not only receive the book, but also several short stories every month too.

Dean Wesley Smith is one of THE most prolific authors I've ever known. He not only writes novels and short stories for his subscribers, but he blogs regularly, writes non-fiction books about writing and publishing AND he holds regular writing workshops.

Compared to all this, doesn't writing a short book seem easy?

The fun part about it is that once you start, writing can become a good addiction.

When you become a prolific writer, life becomes a lot easier too. There's no need to be around other people all the time, or to be always looking for somewhere to go or for the next SBO to entertain you and fill those empty hours.

Instead, there's so much writing to enjoy. Some people find writing to be therapeutic, and some enjoy it so much they just do it for fun.

But if you're serious about being a published author, then you need to be fearless. Write and be published, then do it again.

Don't get too hung up on sales. Write, publish, market, then get on with writing your next book.

Will your first book be good? Who knows. Often It's not your best work, but that doesn't matter.

Your subsequent books will be better. Things always improve with practice.

Once you start writing regularly, you'll settle into your own monthly system of writing and publishing and work it effortlessly.

Writing is what I do and it's how I earn my living. I started writing over 20 years ago and I've never stopped and never wanted to do anything else.

Having a place to write and time to write provides happiness and money.

Carve out your writing time every day/week and guard it ferociously because everything and everyone will try and take it away from you at first. But once they see you're serious, they'll leave you alone to write.

And you can use your writing time to be a consistent monthly author.

Good luck my writing friend.

End

www.ingramcontent.com/pod-product-compliance
Lightning Source LLC
Chambersburg PA
CBHW050320010526
44107CB00055B/2318